FAULKNER

The Major Years c. 1

A CRITICAL STUDY

by Melvin Backman

Indiana University Press   Bloomington & London

In Memory of Dorothy and Maren

Acknowledgments

I am indebted of course to the critics of Faulkner, but I am indebted particularly to those persons who assisted in the preparation of this study. It has been in preparation for twelve years.

The late Richard Chase criticized the manuscript in its early stages. At that time too Lewis Leary and William York Tindall made suggestions for its improvement. In addition, Marston LaFrance made suggestions about the style, Roger Calkins proofread the manuscript, and Charles Penrose of the Clarkson College Library helped in the borrowing of books and periodicals. Later the Division of Research of Clarkson College of Technology provided financial assistance for the acquisition of books. The last readers of the manuscript were my colleagues, Howard Gowen, Konrad Hopkins, and Eugene Williams. To all of these people I am truly grateful.

For permission to reprint parts of this book which appeared as articles, I should like to make the following acknowledgments: to the Purdue Research Foundation for permission to reprint some material of "Faulkner's Sick Heroes: Bayard Sartoris and Quentin Compson," from *Modern Fiction Studies*, 2 (Autumn 1956), 95-108; to M. J. Minard for permission to reprint the chapter on *As I Lay Dying*, which appeared in somewhat different form in *La Revue des Lettres Modernes*, 5 (Hiver 1958-59), 533-554, under the title of "Tandis que j'agonise"; to the *University Review* for permission to reprint (in modified form) the article "Faulkner's *The Wild Palms:* Civilization Against Nature," *University of Kansas City Review*, 28 (March 1962), 199-204;

to the National Council of Teachers of English for permission
to reprint, in the revised chapter on *The Unvanquished*, the
article "Faulkner's 'An Odor of Verbena': Dissent from the
South," from *College English*, 22 (January 1961), 253-256;
and to the Modern Language Association for permission to
reprint "Sutpen and the South: A Study of *Absalom, Absalom!*" from *PMLA*, 80 (December 1965), 596-604, and
"The Wilderness and the Negro in Faulkner's 'The Bear',"
from *PMLA*, 76 (December 1961), 595-600.

I wish to thank the following publishers: Alfred A. Knopf,
Inc., for permission to quote from W. J. Cash, *The Mind of
the South* (Garden City, N.Y., Doubleday, 1954); Random
House, for permission to quote from Irving Howe, *William
Faulkner: A Critical Study* (New York, Random House,
1952); and Kenkyusha Limited for permission to quote from
Faulkner at Nagano, ed. Robert A. Jelliffe (Tokyo, Ken-
kyusha, 1956).

Finally, grateful acknowledgment is made to Random
House for permission to quote from the following works by
William Faulkner: *Sartoris* (New York, Harcourt, Brace,
1929), *The Sound and the Fury* (New York, Modern Library,
1946), *As I Lay Dying* (New York, Modern Library, 1946),
Light in August (New York, Modern Library, 1950), *Ab-
salom, Absalom!* (New York, Modern Library, 1951), *The
Unvanquished* (New York, Random House, 1938), *The Wild
Palms* (New York, Random House, 1939), *The Hamlet* (New
York, Random House, 1940), *Go Down, Moses and Other
Stories* (New York, Random House, 1942).

Preface

The years 1929-1942 were a remarkable period for William Faulkner. In this period he produced the bulk of his work—more than a dozen volumes of stories and novels. He discovered his "own little postage stamp of native soil" and made a world out of Yoknapatawpha County. He peopled it with the Sartorises, Compsons, Tulls, Bundrens, Sutpens, Varners, Snopeses, and McCaslins. He found his major themes and wrote his major works. He did his best work then.

From this period I have selected ten of his novels (or collections of stories) to study both as individual works and as pieces of a larger pattern. Each work, Faulkner has said, has its own design; yet together, he has added, they make another design. I have tried to see both designs. Moving chronologically from work to work, I have considered the relationships existing among the symbols, images, themes, characters, and situations of various books, following attentively the unfolding pattern of the novels of this period. But the primary emphasis has been on each novel as a separate work of art.

Although I prove no thesis and discover no magic key to Faulkner, I do try, by a close analysis of the works and their relationships, to make some sense of them. My purpose is to clarify understanding and sharpen appreciation of Faulkner's works of 1929-1942.

Contents

Faulkner: *The Major Years*

I

Sartoris

Sartoris (1929) introduces one of the central families of Faulkner's Yoknapatawpha novels. Its members are Colonel Sartoris, Civil War leader and founder of the Sartoris clan in Yoknapatawpha County; Aunt Jenny, the erect and indomitable matriarch; crusty old Bayard, son of the Colonel and president of the Jefferson bank; and young Bayard, the twentieth-century heir. On the surface the novel is a family chronicle that nostalgically evokes in the midst of a diminished present the glamorous heroism of a Southern family of the Civil War years. Mingling haphazardly with these memories is a mélange of themes and episodes: the furtive passion of Byron Snopes for Narcissa Benbow; the close affection of brother and sister, Horace and Narcissa Benbow; Horace's involvement with another man's wife, Belle Mitchell; the precarious marriage of Narcissa and young Bayard; Bayard's flight to death; and the various interludes of comedy provided by a boy's blackmailing of Byron, the philandering and the dialogue of old Simon, the doctoring of Bayard by old man Falls, the kindly and courtly teasing of Aunt Jenny by Doc Peabody, and the vigorous attacks of Aunt Jenny upon the servants and the Sartoris men—upon all men, in fact. There is a rich confusion in *Sartoris*.

3

It is a confusion that has invited critical commentary. Irving Howe has said:

> *Sartoris* is the necessary beginning. From the feeling of loss engendered by Bayard Sartoris' postwar malaise, Faulkner will restlessly fall back into the past and move forward to the present. A group of static set-pieces rather than a compact narrative, *Sartoris* reads like a notebook strewn with bits and pieces for a novel still unwritten, as if Faulkner cared only about hurrying it all onto paper. Several of the Yoknapatawpha social groups are summarily introduced: the ebbing patriciate in the Sartorises, the independent farmers in the MacCallums, and then, secondarily, the Snopeses and the Negroes. Though the Yoknapatawpha world is not yet seen distinctly, the feelings it will elicit from its creator lie about in loose profusion, often in excess of what the book itself requires. It is a book heavy with sickness, but neither diagnosis nor cure is suggested; the characteristic tensions of Yoknapatawpha begin to emerge, but still incipient and undefined.[1]

In the endeavor to discover some order and purpose in this confusion, critics have sought to understand the young Sartoris in terms of his family's past. From this point of view, the novel's chief purpose is seen as a contrast between the old and new Sartorises. Some critics, like O'Donnell, go still further and see this novel as the first of Faulkner's works to treat of the social and moral clash between the Sartoris and Snopes families, the clash between traditional and vital morality, on one hand, and self-interest and amorality, on the other.[2] But such critics as Howe and O'Faolain find little "vital morality" in the Sartorises of this novel.[3] Moreover, it

---

[1] Irving Howe, *William Faulkner: A Critical Study* (New York, Random House, 1952), p.28.

[2] See George Marion O'Donnell, "Faulkner's Mythology," in Frederick J. Hoffman and Olga W. Vickery (eds.), *William Faulkner: Three Decades of Criticism* (East Lansing, Michigan State University Press, 1960), pp.82-85.

[3] See Howe, *op. cit.*, pp.28-33; and Sean O'Faolain, *The Vanishing Hero: Studies in Novelists of the Twenties* (London, Eyre & Spottiswoode, 1956), pp.107-109.

is apparent that the Snopeses, whose role in *Sartoris* is entirely minor, are not the antagonists of this work; the deaths of both Bayards, the old banker and his grandson, are in no way attributable to the Snopeses. More important, the chief tension of the novel does not stem from a struggle between classes; it stems from the state of mind of young Bayard Sartoris.

"Proud, rash, violent, doomed,"[4] Bayard is the Byronic hero as well as a member of the "lost generation." Yet his literary ancestry is also Southern romantic: he bears the name of the sixteenth-century Bayard of France whose family history was characterized by violent death and who was known as *"le chevalier sans peur et sans reproche"*[5]; and he bears the name too of his great-granduncle, the other Bayard, the reckless gallant who was aide to Jeb Stuart. Even the name Sartoris—at least for Faulkner—reverberates with connotations of glamorous doom and daring: "there is death in the sound of it [Sartoris], and a glamorous fatality, like silver pennons downrushing at sunset, or a dying fall of horns along the road to Roncevaux."[6] Both Bayard Sartorises, the Civil War cavalry officer and the World War I aviator, are described in the imagery of fallen angels (9, 126) and stars; yet there is a significant difference. The Civil War hero is described in this fashion:

. . . Bayard Sartoris' brief career swept like a shooting star across the dark plain of their mutual remembering and suffering, lighting it with a transient glare like a soundless thunder-clap, leaving a sort of radiance when it died. (18)

. . . against the dark and bloody obscurity of the northern Virginia

---

4 Hyatt H. Waggoner, *William Faulkner: From Jefferson to the World* (Lexington, University of Kentucky Press, 1959), p.25.

5 For this idea I am indebted to Professor Bert Mallet-Prevost Leefmans of Columbia University.

6 William Faulkner, *Sartoris* (New York, Harcourt, Brace, 1929), p.380. This edition is used for all quotations from the novel.

campaigns, Stuart at thirty and Bayard Sartoris at twenty-three
stood briefly like two flaming stars garlanded with Fame's burgeoning laurel and the myrtle and roses of Death. (10)

But the heavens in which the twentieth-century Bayard finds
himself are the "lonely heights of his despair" (288), where
the "cold peaks of savage despair stood bleakly above the
lost valleys among black and savage stars" (205). Darkness
has replaced light, despair has replaced glory.

Invested with the dark, brooding despair of a Byronic
hero, this Bayard of the twentieth century is the novel's central character. Other characters in *Sartoris* may be more appealing or sharply portrayed, but Bayard is the novel's driving force. Of all the characters it is to him Faulkner seems
most deeply committed, as if the character's tension and
despair project something of the author's own state of mind.
In the process of creating Bayard's emotional life, Faulkner
partly works his way out of the boneless, lush style of the
"failed poet," a style which has left its mark upon the novel,
and to have moved toward a concrete, harsh style shaped
by the power of the character's emotion rather than the self-
intoxication of the author's words. When Faulkner was half-
way through *Sartoris,* he discovered, he has said, "that writing is a mighty fine thing; it enabled you to make men stand
on their hind legs and cast a long shadow."[7] Although Bayard may not cast a very long shadow, he is Faulkner's major
concern in the novel.

In the months that followed his return from World War
I, Bayard spent most of his time keeping himself in motion:
driving recklessly along country roads in a fast car, galloping madly through Jefferson on a runaway stallion, and finally
diving to earth in an uncontrollable plane. His need for mo-

---

[7] William Van O'Connor, *The Tangled Fire of William Faulkner*
(Minneapolis, University of Minnesota Press, 1954), p.36.

tion and speed was due not only to the pent up energies of youth, but to a destructive compulsion that derived from an intense yet obscure despair. The despair was planted deep in him. Whatever he tried—drinking, farming, marriage—nothing could uproot it.

The explanation that Faulkner has offered for Bayard's despair—the feeling of guilt and grief over the death of his twin brother, Johnny—seems neither convincing nor adequate. It is true that Johnny was the only one Bayard ever loved; but for the reader Johnny is little more than a name, since the love has not been rendered into life. Moreover, the very nature of Bayard's character—sullen, cold, reserved, and unanalytical—works against a reader's understanding of his inner life. As a result, Bayard's malaise seems in excess of its cause, and its effect upon the novel is oppressive.

The malaise itself is real enough, and the violence it generates understandable. But when Faulkner attributes Bayard's violence to the "glamorous fatality" of the Sartoris heritage, he strikes a false note. Intentionally or not, he confuses malaise with doom, as if his power and will to explore reality were surrendering to his need to romanticize it. The tendency to indulge in romantic glorification or sentimentality is a serious flaw in *Sartoris*. It blunts the author's sense of reality, reduces his control over the material, and diffuses the effect of the novel. The result is a self-defeating ambivalence. This ambivalence is evident, for example, in Faulkner's treatment of the Civil War and the Sartorises of that period, the Colonel and his brother Bayard. On one hand, Aunt Jenny serves as an ironic commentator on the "heritage of humorless and fustian vainglory" (374), as she and occasionally Will Falls or Simon deflate the Sartoris and Civil War legends; on the other hand, even Aunt Jenny, as well as old man Falls and Simon, perpetuate the legends.

In a mood of nostalgic pride and melancholy reverie, these survivors of the Old South turn back to self-entranced dreams of legendary men and days; with the help of soft music, fire-light, musky chests, an old keepsake, and the soaring "verbal wings" (172) of the author's rhetoric, they recall the glories of the past. Aunt Jenny turns to the ghosts of Jeb Stuart and her brother Bayard; Simon and Will Falls turn to the Colonel's ghost.

Despite the romantic trappings, there is a core of reality to *Sartoris:* it is the death wish of Bayard. From his first appearance in the story, the desire for death struggles against his will to live. Symptomatic of the death wish are his wild automobile rides, violent accidents, and heavy drinking; indicative of his will to live are his farming of the land and his marriage to Narcissa. But his unresting despair has cut him off from the quiet sober rhythms of farming, and the coldness of his heart has doomed the marriage from its be-ginning. His inability to love is part of a neurotic estrange-ment from man and life itself. Hence, an early violent death seems inevitable for Bayard. Notwithstanding the inevitabil-ity, a struggle between the will to live and the desire to die persists in Bayard and imparts to the novel its Faulknerian tension.

At the death of his grandfather, young Bayard, driven by his sense of guilt and by despair, flees to the pine woods of his past: to the MacCallum farm where he had often stayed as a boy. As the malaise of Bayard is set in moving counter-point against the natural idyll of the MacCallum family, the writing takes on power and poetry. The MacCallums, the old patriarch and his six sons, are the family isolated from our world, bound in simple affection and living close to nature. Their home is a refuge of warmth and light, the hearth its symbol:

The fire crackled and swirled; from time to time Stuart, nearest the wood-box, put another log on. The dog at the old man's feet dreamed, snuffed; soft ashes swirled on the hearth at its nose and it sneezed, waking itself, and raised its head and blinked up at the old man's face, then dozed again. They sat without words and with very little movement, their grave, aquiline faces as though carved by the firelight out of the shadowy darkness, shaped by a single thought and smoothed and colored by the same hand. (318)

Behind the reserved and grave mien of the MacCallums there is a shared love, behind the silence a rare repose. One senses the absoluteness of their mutual loyalty, the straightness and simplicity of their code. Their rock is the father.[8]

But Bayard's despair—described as cold, dark, savage, and bleak—cuts him off from the light and warmth and pulls him toward death. "He was shaking slowly and steadily with cold; beneath his hands his flesh was rough and without sensation; yet still it jerked and jerked as though something within the dead envelope of him strove to free itself" (323). On Christmas eve he rode away from the MacCallum home into the cold dark woods of the western hills. He found a night's lodging in a Negro cabin, and on Christmas day he was driven to the station. There amid the cheerful people, the exploding firecrackers, and the arcing rockets, never had Bayard seemed more alien and alone as he waited for the train that would carry him to death.

Less important in the novel than Bayard is Horace Ben-

---

[8] Tall, lean, and straight as an Indian, old MacCallum towers a head above his sons, with the exception of Buddy. Buddy is the youngest son; possessing the name, stature, and features of his father, he is the true heir. These two, father and son, are the first of Faulkner's natural men: physically they are like the tall convict of *The Wild Palms* and Jewel Bundren of *As I Lay Dying*, who are similarly described as tall, grave, and Indian-like. Tallness, in fact, seems generally associated by Faulkner with masculinity.

bow, who is both a foil and complement to the young Sartoris. Bayard is cold and inexpressive, Horace affectionate
and voluble. Bayard is in love with violence, Horace with a
chaste serenity. Against Bayard's precariously leashed despair and explosive destructiveness, Horace's passivity and
gentle melancholy seem weak and effeminate. Yet both
share a sense of estrangement from life, though Horace's
estrangement is less extreme than Bayard's because his personality is less extreme. Unlike Bayard he is submissive
rather than assertive. He does not confront life; he tends to
evade it. Rooted in his pleasure of making beautiful sounds
out of words or beautiful shapes out of glass is the need to
withdraw and escape from the arena of life. His "thin, nerve-
sick face" (173) mirrors an abiding sense of futility. He is
an unfulfilled poet and idealist willing to deceive himself
and willing to purchase peace at the expense of life.

This is reflected in the pattern of his life. Unlike the active
and masculine Bayard, he served in the war as a Red Cross
worker. Bayard returned from the war bearing a burden
of guilt for his brother's death; Horace returned with a glass
blower's equipment. The "chastely serene" (182) vases Horace makes suggest the kind of peace he is seeking; they are
associated with his sister, whom he addresses as "'thou still
unravished bride of quietness'" (182, 352). His sister's love
is deeply reassuring to him:

> Narcissa reached her hand beneath the table and touched her
> brother's knee again. "I *am* glad you're home, Horry."
> He looked at her quickly, and the cloud faded from his face
> as suddenly as it had come, and his spirit slipped, like a swimmer
> into a tideless sea, into the serene constancy of her affection
> again. (175)

His love for his sister is regressive and self-destructive. On
the other hand, his adulterous love for Belle Mitchell is

equally self-destructive, because in the uneasy union of these two opposed natures the finer but weaker nature is doomed. On the eve of Horace's marriage with Belle, his mind recalls an incident out of the past, like a warning from his unconscious:

Belle had freed her mouth, and for a moment, her body still against his, she held his face in her two hands and stared at him with intent, questioning eyes. "Have you plenty of money, Horace?" And "Yes," he had answered immediately, "of course I have." And then Belle again, enveloping him like a rich and fatal drug, like a motionless and cloying sea in which he watched himself drown. (257)

Reminding us of the metaphor that describes Horace's love for his sister, this image of man's drowning in the sea of woman, so to speak, characterizes Horace Benbow. It seems significant that what is only a figure of speech for Horace Benbow will become actuality for Quentin Compson in *The Sound and the Fury.*

In his estrangement, then, Horace serves as an unheroic complement to the more romantic Bayard. It is Bayard, not Horace, who—solitary and proud, ridden by guilt and despair—bears his estrangement aloft as if it were a pennant. The young generation in *Sartoris* are characterized chiefly by their alienation; the old—there is no middle generation— by their vigor, humor, colorfulness, and nostalgia. The portraits of the old are drawn with sympathy and detail, as if they derive from cherished memories; those of the young are flat and abbreviated, as if they derive from a present too perilously close. The present is a time of despair and malaise, the past a time of heroism and purpose. But it is the present, as signified by Bayard and Horace, that seems to have touched the author's heart more deeply.

The central theme of *Sartoris* is the theme of the alienated self. Yet at the time of the writing of the novel Faulkner was apparently not quite ready to explore the theme's full reality, as if he could not break through certain inner defenses. Consequently the novel moves in too many directions, creating a confusion of theme and plot. It is an unsuccessful but important novel, since it discovered for its author the Yoknapatawpha material and led directly to the creation of his finest novel, *The Sound and the Fury*. In *The Sound and the Fury* Faulkner was to penetrate deeply into the inner life of his estranged hero and to unfold the tragic complexity of the human heart.

2

The Sound and the Fury

With *The Sound and the Fury* (1929), William Faulkner the artist came of age. He produced his masterpiece—
one of the great tragic novels of the twentieth century. He
proved himself a master in his command of a difficult technique, in his control of language, and in the highly original
organization of his material. Taking Joyce's stream-of-
consciousness technique, Faulkner exploited it in his own
way. He may have lacked the intellectuality and knowledge,
literary and religious, of Joyce, but he possessed his own
emotional and imaginative powers. In the dialogue and interior monologues of his characters, Faulkner showed a keen
ear for the sound of people's voices and an even keener sensitivity to the quality of their thoughts and feelings. *The
Sound and the Fury* demonstrates a remarkable power of
characterization. There are few passages in modern literature that compare with Mrs. Compson's monologue or the
interior monologues of Jason in their terse power to render
into life the mind and personality of a character.

To give structure to his stream-of-consciousness novel,
Faulkner did not, like Joyce, make use of a myth; instead,
he organized his work by mood and theme, as if it were a
musical composition. Concentrating on a member of the

Compson family, each section develops a separate tonal movement as well as a separate perspective. The novel moves with affecting contrast from the simple sensations of Benjy to the complex emotions and introversion of Quentin, then to the strident, violent anger of Jason, and finally to the reassuring calm of Dilsey. Certain themes—love, time, and the world's destruction of innocence—are part of each section. Certain symbols—honeysuckle, water, the stain, trees, flowers, the mirror, fire, and light—run like musical motifs through the novel; they fuse, intensify, heighten, and enrich the novel's emotion and meaning. Even the apparent randomness and fragmentary quality of the stream of consciousness are generally a meaningful part of a character's personality or state of mind. Each section, then, has its own ordered movement; each movement combines in this polyphonic composition to tell the story of the fall of the House of Compson.

Faulkner, it has been said, spent three years in composing this work. The depth and density of its created life testify to a long, intense concentration of mind and heart. Yet for all its depth and complexity, the novel does not seem labored. Despite the sudden shifts of time and the fragmentary, unorthodox narration of the story, the scenes flow and fuse like parts of a fugue. Underlying and uniting the scenes' fragments is a mood of compassion and despair. *The Sound and the Fury* is a deeply felt and deeply moving work that demonstrates an artist's superb intuitive control of his material. The language—the simple concreteness and muted lyricism of the Benjy section, the racy verve of Jason's interior monologues, and the "pictorial majesty"[1] of the author's own style in the Dilsey section—evolves naturally out

---

[1] Irving Howe, *William Faulkner: A Critical Study*, p.26.

of situation, mood, and character. The style is unmannered
and uncluttered. In this work Faulkner found his voice by
losing himself, as if, like the inspired Reverend Shegog in
the Negro church, "he was nothing and they [the audience]
were nothing and there was not even a voice but instead
their hearts were speaking to one another" (310).[2]

Faulkner has described *The Sound and the Fury* as the
novel "which caused me the most anguish . . . the one that
I feel most tender toward,"[3] the one into which I have "written my guts."[4] Even long after publication the story continued to plague the author until, about sixteen years later,
he wrote an appendix in "the final effort to get the story told
and off my mind, so that I myself could have some peace
from it."[5] The anguish of the novel is centered in Quentin
Compson. The author is intimately and deeply involved
with his protagonist's plight, as most critics have recognized.
William Van O'Connor has observed, "It could well be that
in Quentin one finds the central issue of the novel."[6] Irving
Howe has commented, however, on the limitations of the
Quentin section:

The Quentin section abruptly reduces the scope of the novel to a
problem that is "special" in a clinical sense and not necessarily an
equivalent or derivative of the Compson history. Where Benjy
recalls a world, Quentin nurses an obsession. The exact nature of

---

[2] The Modern Library edition (1946) of *The Sound and the Fury* is
used for all quotations from the text.
[3] *Faulkner at Nagano,* ed. Robert A. Jelliffe (Tokyo, Kenkyusha
Press, 1956), p.103.
[4] William Faulkner, Introduction to *Sanctuary* (New York, Modern
Library, 1932), p.vi.
[5] Jean Stein, "William Faulkner: An Interview," in Frederick J.
Hoffman and Olga W. Vickery (eds.), *William Faulkner: Three
Decades of Criticism,* p.74.
[6] William Van O'Connor, *The Tangled Fire of William Faulkner,*
p.39.

this obsession is not easy to determine: it is partly a problem of
his sexual life and partly a problem in family or caste pride.[7]

Howe's observation that the Quentin section creates a narrow, obsessional world is right, yet the role played by Quentin is crucial to *The Sound and the Fury*. The Quentin
section, after all, covers one-third of the novel's pages and
is the longest of the four sections. More important, Quentin's
neurotic estrangement from life affects, in different ways,
the other sections of the novel and shapes the novel's mood
and meaning. What Quentin represents is central not only
to *The Sound and the Fury* but to others of Faulkner's novels
affected by the theme of alienation. For this reason, an
attempt to determine the nature of Quentin's alienation and
its relationship to the parts and the whole of the novel needs
to be made.

Although the Quentin section is dated June 2, 1910, it is
chiefly concerned with Quentin's obsessive recall of the
scenes relating to the Dalton Ames episode in the summer
of 1909 and Caddy's wedding in April 1910. The actual
events of this day, Quentin's last, are subordinated to the
charged memories and disturbed emotions that break into
his consciousness. In a strange, fuguelike manner the present
always leads back to the past. The effect is to split Quentin
in two: on the surface, he goes through the external motions
of living, as though performing a ritual carefully yet de-
tachedly; all the while, however, his emotional and mental
life are occupied by the past. The past is broken into seemingly disjointed fragments that push again and again into
his consciousness, but at times, like the sudden revelation
of a dream, they coalesce into a vivid, harrowing scene.
Quentin's stream of consciousness achieves a remarkable
effect: at the same time that he struggles against certain

---

[7] Howe, pp.119-120.

memories, as if he wished to obliterate them from his consciousness, he seems compelled to relive them. The broken sequence of his memories and thoughts conveys a sense of disintegration as well as a reluctance to recall painful memories; their repetition and circling movement suggest a compulsive return to the source of a deep-rooted frustration.

At the beginning of the section Quentin's memories turn back to Caddy's wedding. There is a brief, sharp vision of Caddy in her wedding dress, veil and roses, as she ran out of the mirror to Benjy. Benjy was *"lying on the ground under the window bellowing* He took one look at her and knew. Out of the mouths of the babes" (119). Benjy sensed the "sin" behind Caddy's marriage; his bellowing was his protest. That Benjy had this awareness has been demonstrated in those incidents (of the first section) in which Benjy moaned or bellowed his disapproval of Caddy for wearing perfume (59-62), for kissing boys (65-67), and later for making love with Dalton Ames (87-88, 143, 168). These scenes chart the course of Caddy's sexual life as well as the decline of Benjy's effectiveness as her moral arbiter. In the first two scenes Benjy stirred her sense of shame so that she washed off the "taint" and once again smelled like trees; in the third scene Benjy cried in vain and she ran from him; at the wedding Benjy got drunk and bellowed his disapproval outside. Benjy was protesting against Caddy's sexuality because it threatened to deprive him of Caddy's love. When Caddy smelled like trees he could return to the security of their childhood years.

Quentin, as his frequent remembrance of Benjy's outcry against Caddy's marriage implies, shared some of Benjy's feelings, though his own feelings were complicated and introverted. He attacked Caddy's choice of husband on the grounds that Herbert Head was a blackguard, yet he was apparently more disturbed by Caddy's loss of honor than by

Head's lack of scruples. Underlying Quentin's disturbed
antagonism to Caddy's marriage is a complex brother-sister
relationship that had its roots in their childhood and in
the negativity of their mother.

There are almost no scenes in the novel depicting any relationship between Quentin and his mother. The image of
his mother which emerges from his thoughts and memories
is essentially hostile and critical. In her striking monologue
that Quentin re-creates (121-123), she stands revealed in
her terrible self-centeredness and hypocrisy. A weak, whin-
ing, cold woman, she was imprisoned in self-pity and took
refuge in neurasthenia. Her Christianity consisted of a small
martyr complex and a shabbily genteel concern about "virtue." Incapable of love, sacrifice, or charity, she failed her
family as mother. For the love she did not provide, Quentin
turned to his sister. But the love that grew between brother
and sister was subject to invasion by sex.

Associated with sex is the symbol of the stain. The central
and germinal image from which *The Sound and the Fury*
originated, Faulkner has said on several occasions, is the
image of the stained bottom of a little girl's drawers.

It [*The Sound and the Fury*] began with a mental picture. I
didn't realize at the time it was symbolical. The picture was of
the muddy seat of a little girl's drawers in a pear tree, where she
could see through a window where her grandmother's funeral
was taking place and report what was happening to her brothers
on the ground below. By the time I explained who they were
and what they were doing and how her pants got muddy, I
realized it would be impossible to get all of it into a short story
and that it would have to be a book.[8]

---

[8] Faulkner made this explanation in 1956 in an interview by Jean
Stein (*Three Decades of Criticism*, p.73). He made similar comments
at other times; see Frederick L. Gwynn and Joseph L. Blotner (eds.),
*Faulkner in the University: Class Conferences at the University of
Virginia 1957-1958* (Charlottesville, University of Virginia Press, 1959),
pp.1, 31.

This image has to do with the childhood scene of the evening of Damuddy's death (about 1898) when Caddy, despite Quentin's objections, took off her dress to wade in the branch and muddied her drawers. On the children's return to the house, Caddy climbed a tree in order to see into the parlor window. Dilsey came out and, looking up at the stained bottom, said, " 'You, Satan. . . . Come down from there' " (64). Later that evening Dilsey scrubbed the stain, but it would not come off. The stain seems intended as a portent of Caddy's sexuality and promiscuity. Yet its symbolism seems still more significant, as if Faulkner were associating Caddy's stained bottom with Satan and the forbidden tree in Eden, as if he were associating her stain with original sin. Paradoxically, Caddy was the tree of life for Benjy, but for Quentin she would prove the fatal tree of knowledge.

Sex invaded their love when Caddy and Quentin were in their early youth. Quentin was reliving that past as he walked with the little Italian girl he called sister in the alien countryside of Cambridge—sometimes along the river "running swift and peaceful in the secret shade" (154), sometimes through empty streets or back lanes, searching for a home they never found. This is the background against which the past is evoked; yet as in a dream past and present flow strangely one into the other, eliciting feelings and imparting meanings only darkly understood.

As Quentin watched the little girl chew steadily on the ratlike cake and the ice cream, he remembered his father's words:

Because women so delicate so mysterious Father said. Delicate equilibrium of periodical filth between two moons balanced. Moons he said full and yellow as harvest moons her hips thighs. Outside outside of them always but. Yellow. Feetsoles with walking like. Then know that some man that all those mysterious and imperious concealed. With all that inside of them shapes an outward suavity waiting for a touch to. Liquid putrefaction like drowned things floating like pale rubber flabbily filled getting the odour of honeysuckle all mixed up. (147)

They continued their journey on a lane that led to a woodlot where were vines and creepers; at home, thought Quentin, there would be honeysuckle.

Coming and coming especially in the dusk when it rained, getting honeysuckle all mixed up in it as though it were not enough without that, not unbearable enough. *What did you let him for kiss kiss* (152)

And he was back in the past: he was slapping Caddy for kissing the boy and was scouring her head in the grass; he was hugging the dirty Natalie in the empty barn and listening to the rat in the crib and to the rain coming hard upon the roof[9]; he was with Caddy again, outside in the cold rain, and was fighting with her and smearing her with the foul mud of the hogwallow; and then they went to the branch to wash it off. Somewhere in the woods "beyond the broken and infrequent slanting of sunlight" (154), a bird was whistling. He looked at the little Italian girl.

"Poor kid, you're just a girl." Little flowers grew among the moss, littler than I had ever seen. "You're just a girl. Poor kid." There was a path, curving along beside the water. Then the water was still again, dark and still and swift. "Nothing but a girl. Poor Sister." (157)

A strangely evocative scene, it is heavy with symbolic and allegorical implications. Most apparent is the dreamlike association of the little girl with Caddy. For Quentin both sisters were lost, and despite his help neither could find her way home. The little girl, described frequently as black and occa-

---

[9] The rat in the crib, as well as the sound of invisible dripping, will later be part of the setting for the rape of Temple Drake in *Sanctuary*.

sionally as dirty, has been linked with Quentin's memories of
early sexual experiences, of the dirty Natalie, and of the
muddy Caddy, and with his morbid thoughts about the mysterious delicate filth of women. In one sense, the present, because of the little girl's association with Caddy and of the
river with the branch, has functioned as a reminder of a
disturbing past and a repelling sexuality. In another sense,
the girl reminded Quentin of the Caddy of childhood: she
was the little sister, the poor kid who would be transformed
by time, so to speak, from "little pale flowers" (155) to roses
"cunning and serene" (96),[10] from Saint Francis' little flowers of innocence to Baudelaire's flowers of evil. Nevertheless,
the most deeply felt symbolism of this scene may well be not
that of sex or childhood but of death. In the back of Quentin's mind was a constant awareness of the river "running
swift and peaceful in the secret shade" (154);[11] almost always by his side and associated with the promise of death,
the river is a dominant presence in this scene. Associated with
the river too is the little girl, who is described many times as
black and still or "black and secret and friendly" (154).[12]
Quentin Compson, Faulkner seems to be saying, has lost his
sister Caddy but has found—in the words of Saint Francis—
his "Little Sister Death" (96).

However—when the girl's brother wildly attacked Quentin, when Quentin was arrested and fined in a farcical trial
for having "molested" the little girl, and when Spoade, the
Harvard senior from South Carolina, commented amusingly

---

[10] For Quentin the roses that adorn Caddy the bride symbolize "not
virgin" (96); they seem symbolic too, as Mrs. Vickery has observed, of
Caddy's "promiscuity and her 'sin' made socially respectable" (*The
Novels of William Faulkner,* Baton Rouge, Louisiana State University
Press, 1959, p.41).

[11] See also pp.155, 157 and 159.

[12] See also pp.147, 148, 149, 151, 152 and 157.

on Quentin's "nefarious" work—the episode ends inconclusively and the mood shifts to that of bitter-sweet irony and farce. We are not ready yet for Quentin's suicide; we need the explanation first. The explanation, which has been deliberately withheld, comes in the Dalton Ames episode—fragment by fragment. The fragments begin to piece together, the emotion intensifies, and the Quentin section mounts to its climax.

Like Eliot's interweaving of Prufrock's reveries with the women's talk of Michelangelo, Faulkner artfully interweaves Quentin's thoughts and memories with the chatter of Mrs. Bland and of the others in the car about gentlemen and wine, a mint julep recipe, and Gerald's rowing suit. Then Gerald's oars seemed to blur in Quentin's mind with the running of Caddy:

with one hand he could lift her to his shoulder and run with her running Running. . . . running the beast with two backs and she blurred in the winking oars running the swine of Euboeleus running coupled within how many Caddy. . . . I dont know too many. . . . Father I have committed. . . . (167)

The image of Dalton running as he carried Caddy merges with Iago's gross image of copulation and with the running of swine by the swineherd who witnessed the rape and abduction of Persephone by Hades.[13] The reference to swine recalls the scene in the hogwallow where Quentin befouled Caddy and himself. The accumulated effect of the imagery of these scenes creates a feeling of sexual nausea and suggests that Quentin was experiencing a deep-rooted revulsion from sex. He seemed to be experiencing too a strong sense of separation, as if, in some fundamental way, he were cut off from the others.

---

[13] For Iago's image, see *Othello*, I, i, 118. For another Faulkner image that joins swine and sex, see p.195.

Caddy's "poor Quentin youve never done that have you" goaded him into a revealing outburst:

you thought it was them but it was me listen I fooled you all the time it was me you thought I was in the house where that damn honeysuckle trying not to think the swing the cedars the secret surges the breathing locked drinking the wild breath yes Yes Yes yes (167)

It was in the hammock swing by the cedars that Caddy, especially after her affair with Dalton Ames was broken off in the summer of 1909, used to take her lovers. Apparently Quentin, as he lay hidden in the honeysuckle close by, sought to identify with Caddy's lovers in the sexual act, as if by the very desperation of his will and wish he could force reality out of fantasy. Yet there were other forces in Quentin stronger than his desire to identify with her lovers: his love and hatred of Caddy, his hatred of her lovers and of the act itself, his morbid idealism, and his death wish. The essential part of Quentin sought to thwart rather than to unite with Caddy's sexuality. In one sense, this may be explained as love struggling against lust; yet, in another sense, this may be explained as impotence attacking sexual potency. Certainly Quentin, jokingly called Shreve's wife and the model youth by Spoade, showed little sexual desire in his twenty years of life. It is this sense of impotence—psychic and, to some extent, physical, since both are integrally related and mutually interactive—which, combined with his love for Caddy, seems to underlie Quentin's idealism and desire for death.

The disclosure of this impotence, in the scene with Caddy at the branch and with Dalton at the bridge, is the climax of the Quentin section. It is these two scenes toward which the fragments of Quentin's compulsive, tortured memory have been building; it is these scenes which seem the most deeply felt and passionately rendered. A few nights before the meet-

ing with Dalton Ames, Quentin ran after Caddy to the
branch; she had run from the cries of Benjy and was lying in
the water, the water flowing futilely about her hips, the air
drizzling with honeysuckle. So oppressive was the effect of
honeysuckle upon Quentin that it seemed to draw the very
breath out of his lungs. Associated with Caddy's lovemaking
in the swing by the cedars, honeysuckle seemed to rake open
the wound of his memories of her promiscuity and his own
humiliation and failure.

> Caddy you hate him dont you
> she moved my hand up against her throat her heart was ham-
> mering there
> poor Quentin
> her face looked at the sky it was low so low that all smells and
> sounds of night seemed to have been crowded down like under
> a slack tent especially the honeysuckle it had got into my breath-
> ing it was on her face and throat like paint her blood pounded
> against my hand I was leaning on my other arm it began to jerk
> and jump and I had to pant to get any air at all out of that thick
> grey honeysuckle (169-170)

> youve never done that have you
> what done what
> that what I have what I did
> yes yes lots of times with lots of girls
> then I was crying her hand touched me again and I was crying
> against her damp blouse then she lying on her back looking past
> my head into the sky I could see a rim of white under her irises
> I opened my knife (170)

But Quentin could do nothing.

Then Dalton Ames came, tall and assured, and she went to
him. Three days later Quentin met him by arrangement at
the bridge over the creek. The sun was slanting in broken
light, a bird was singing somewhere in the woods, and he
could hear the sound of the water.

Ill give you until sundown to leave town

.   .   .   .

listen no good taking it so hard its not your fault kid it would
have been some other fellow
   did you ever have a sister did you
   no but theyre all bitches (178-179)

Quentin tried to hit him then, but Dalton caught his wrists
and Quentin lost consciousness. He awoke to the sound of the
bird and the water and to the broken sunlight across his eyes.
Caddy came to him, and he asked her, "Do you love him?"
In answer she held his hand to her throat to feel the surge
of her blood at the sound of "Dalton Ames." "Her face looked
off into the trees where the sun slanted and where the
bird . . ." (182)

Now the pieces begin to fall in place. This combination of
symbols—the bird, water, and broken sunlight—which runs
like a strangely familiar and disturbing melody through the
crucial scenes with Caddy and Dalton was first introduced
to the reader in the scene in which Quentin walked along
the river with the little Italian girl:[14]

There was a bird somewhere in the woods, beyond the broken
and infrequent slanting of sunlight.

.   .   .   .

The bird whistled again, invisible, a sound meaningless and
profound, inflexionless, ceasing as though cut off with the blow
of a knife, and again, and that sense of water swift and peaceful
above secret places, felt, not seen not heard. (154-155)

While the trial proceeded, Quentin's attention was on the
slanting sunlight, as if he were apart from the proceedings
(163); when he broke into hysteria in the Bland car, his
thoughts were with the past that was obliterating the present

---

[14] For Faulkner's development of this motif, see, in particular, pp.
154-155, 159, 163, 166, 179, 180, 181, 182 and 187.

—with the slanting afternoon, the bird, and the water (166). Once again, as Gerald Bland blurred into Dalton Ames, he was trying to fight Dalton, as if he were driven by a desperate need to undo his rejection and humiliation as well as by a masochistic need to relive his failure and to be punished. He lost consciousness, but only after Gerald had punished him bloodily. When he awoke, the sun had become a "round blob of twilight wobbling . . . like a fading balloon" (182) in the water of the basin brought him by Shreve. Only a fading reflection in water, the light was going out of Quentin's world; the meaningless whistle of the solitary bird was yielding to the stillness of the water.

Quentin had to fight Dalton, not only because Dalton had taken his sister's honor but because Dalton had uttered and demonstrated what Quentin's mind knew as truth but what his heart would not accept: that Caddy was a bitch. He could not give her up, for she was the one he loved. Rooted in a past to which Quentin felt he had to return, his love for her is essentially regressive. His love suggests a basic failure in Quentin—the inability to accept change and confront life; nevertheless, it is real. For Quentin the loss of Caddy was tragic because there was no one else to whom he could turn. One brother was an idiot, the other was Jason, his mother was no mother, and his father—having found a refuge in fatalism, pessimism, and alcoholism—could bring his son neither light nor strength.

As Quentin waited for the trolley to take him back to Harvard, he saw "the last light supine and tranquil upon tide-flats like pieces of broken mirror" (188), and he remembered how Benjy had found a "refuge unfailing" (188-189) in the mirror of the past. When Quentin returned to his room, the twilight had become darkness. For a moment, while he was cleaning the blood from his vest, he thought, *"If I'd just had*

a mother so I could say Mother Mother" (190). He recalled
a picture in a book that he and his sister and brothers had
had when they were little, a picture of "a dark place into
which a single weak ray of light came slanting upon two faces
lifted out of the shadow. . . . The dungeon was Mother herself she and Father upward into weak light holding hands
and us lost somewhere below even them without even a ray
of light" (191). He went on with his preparations: carefully,
as if he were performing a final purifying ritual, he washed
himself, cleaned his clothes so that the stain did not show in
the mirror, and brushed his teeth. When the bells tolled the
last hour of night, he was ready to leave the room for the
bridge where he had hidden the flatirons. At a bridge he
had lost Caddy to Dalton; now at a bridge he would find
death by water.

On the surface Quentin's reason for suicide is the loss of
his sister's honor. It has been traditional, of course, for the
Southerner to idealize and defend Southern womanhood.
From this point of view one may regard Caddy as symbolic
of the lost honor of the Compson family or, in a larger sense,
of a dying aristocracy, and Quentin as its last defender. But
this explanation is partial, at best. His obsession with his sister's chastity derives largely, as Irving Howe has noted, from
a personal rather than a cultural situation, although it is
entirely possible that the Southern code, the puritan view of
sex, and the Christian attitude to celibacy and martyrdom
have contributed to the characterization of Quentin Compson. The ultimate reason for Quentin's suicide is the loss of
Caddy to Dalton. It was not so much the gross materialism
of Herbert Head that defeated Quentin as the sexual potency
of Dalton Ames. Like Benjy, he recoiled from sex, for it would
destroy the private paradise he had tried to create from his
attachment to Caddy. His obsession with her chastity, as well

as his own deficiency of sexual desire, seems for the most part
the consequence of his regressive love for her. The regres-
siveness and the psychic impotence induced certain rationalizations: honor and morality. Desperately Quentin needed to
believe in the sinfulness of Caddy's acts and the moral recti-
tude of his judgment in order to establish the truth of his
kind of love. His unconvincing claim that he had committed
incest with his sister was another desperate attempt to "isolate her out of the loud world" (195) and, as his father saw,
to "sublimate a piece of natural human folly into a horror and
then exorcise it with truth" (195).

But Quentin should not be taken at face value. Although
Faulkner has made some use of Quentin's father to provide a
detached and ironic perspective on his son, Quentin's own
estimate of himself generally dominates the second section.
Faulkner identifies too much with his protagonist and does
not always " 'detect' one of his own characters."[15] What may
annoy or disturb some readers is the unrelieved morbidity of
Quentin's outlook. Some critics, who have judged the Quentin section as the least successful, regard Quentin as a clinical
case; others tend to take his moral and philosophical abstractions at face value.[16] Quentin's abstractions seem to me to be
chiefly rationalizations of inadequacy, as well as a means of
putting distance between himself and deeply troubling experiences. Admittedly, because of his disturbed state of mind,
Quentin is a risk in a stream-of-consciousness novel; but if he
is central to the novel, he is a necessary risk.

---

[15] This is Eliot's phrase commenting on the relationship between
Henry James and his character Rowland in *Roderick Hudson;* see T. S.
Eliot, "Henry James," in Edmund Wilson (ed.), *The Shock of Recogni-
tion* (New York, Doubleday, 1943), p.864.

[16] For examples of the former criticism, see Howe, pp.39-40, 118-
123, and Richard Chase, *The American Novel and Its Tradition*
(Doubleday, 1957), pp.222-223, 228-230; for an example of the latter
criticism, see Hyatt H. Waggoner, *William Faulkner: From Jefferson to
the World,* pp.47-53.

One might compare Quentin with Eliot's Prufrock, another weak and sensitive intellectual. Both characters regarded themselves through their knowledge of great religious and literary personalities. Quentin alluded often to Saint Francis and Jesus,[17] and apparently compared himself with Prince Hamlet, another sensitive introvert involved with incest and suicide. Prufrock compared himself in his reveries with John the Baptist, Lazarus, and Hamlet, although he recognized that he could not qualify for a prince or a saint but only for a ridiculous Polonius. Quentin would not give up trying to be something of a saint, martyr, or a Prince Hamlet. Prufrock possesses what Quentin lacks—a fairly realistic self-awareness; Quentin possesses what Prufrock lacks—an emotional commitment to life. Despite his dreams of "sea-girls wreathed with seaweed red and brown," Prufrock is emotionally dead; despite his neurosis and death-wish, Quentin is alive.

"Once a bitch always a bitch" (198): so begins the Jason section. The transition from the Quentin section is abrupt. The change in tone, theme, and the author's relation to his character is extreme. Moreover, the Jason section is dominated by the present, whereas the emotional life of Benjy and Quentin was dominated by the past. This section tells about both Jason and the family. The decline and fall of the House of Compson emerges definitely as the novel's subject. Of the three sons through whom Faulkner has told the story of the Compson family, Jason is the one to whom Faulkner is most hostile. Although Jason may have been conceived out of hostility, his impact upon the reader is partly that of a comic character—a comic villain. After the morbidity and introversion of Quentin, the harsh wit and angry violence of Jason provide a sudden, welcome release through comedy. There is a double-edged humor in the rich sarcasm that

---

[17] See pp.96, 98, 99, 135, 189, 190 and 194.

flows naturally and easily out of Jason's permanent discontent, for he is both the maker and the butt of the satire. As his
own anger, frustration, and frantic activity rise in tone and
tempo, the comedy moves swiftly to its climax. When Jason
finally fails in the pursuit of his money, earned as well as
stolen, the comedy is complete. Some of Faulkner's finest
comedy is found in this brilliant satire of Jason, the seeker of
the golden fleece.

Jason is more than a comic character. He is the major
antagonist in this moral tale of a deteriorating family. The
family was besieged by hypochondria, alcoholism, idiocy, suicide, promiscuity, and the threat of incest. But the destruction of the family ultimately rests upon the destruction of
love. The problem of love dominates all sections of the novel.
The split in the Compson family—the Bascombs (Mother
and Jason) against the Compsons (Father, Quentin, Caddy,
and Benjy)—was the result of the love that united the four
and of the lovelessness that united the two. Unable to love,
Jason and Mrs. Compson have become the antagonists of
those who do love. They are, so to speak, the negative and
positive poles of a power for evil: Mrs. Compson fails to provide love, Jason hates. Hate is the chief source of Jason's
energy. He hates and damns them all—"niggers," "jews,"
Babe Ruth, the Yankees, the carnival show, his employer, his
niece, his sister, Dilsey, and his family. Jason, according to
Faulkner, is the most vicious character he has ever created.[18]
Jason's antagonism to his brothers and sister, as well as his
meanness and avarice, may be noticed in his earliest years.
Of all the Compson children he was the least sympathetic.
Basically Caddy was loving and generous, Quentin kind and
idealistic, and Benjy helpless. But Jason neither gave nor re-

---

[18] *Faulkner at Nagano,* p.104.

ceived love. For him love was a commodity, as may be seen by the practical business arrangement he made with his whore. He did not recognize any other kind of love; in fact, he plotted against love. For years he had maliciously and vengefully frustrated Caddy's concern for her daughter. By spiteful treatment he had helped, as his niece rightly claimed, to make her into a bitch; his niece's sexual promiscuity was her way of realizing love and of rebelling against Jason. Despite his utter lack of compassion and his extraordinary talent for hating, Jason remains—because of Faulkner's superbly realistic portrayal—convincingly human.

He is human in another sense. Hypocrite, liar, forger, thief, featherer of his own nest, perpetual malcontent, and congenital hater, he had made, nevertheless, the essential accommodation: he accepted his society. Like his mother, he was concerned not with virtue but with propriety. His niece's promiscuity did not really faze him—how could it since he respected nothing more than "a good honest whore"? (251)— but the publicness of her behavior did vex him sorely. He is human too, flagrantly and irrationally, in his inconsistencies, self-contradictions, and blind hypocrisies. Money, he said, had no value (212), but he spent his life hoarding it; he condemned Earl for being satisfied with a paltry eight percent profit but attacked the "eastern jews" for profiteering; he spent a large part of his working day chasing after his niece but berated old Job for malingering; and he waxed with the honest rage of the hypocrite over his niece's theft and lies. No, Jason is not rational, as critics have said; nor is he as shrewd as he and others have claimed. A prisoner of unreasonable angers, he drove up and down the country roads in frantic pursuit of his niece until migraine headaches and a little old man forced him to return home defeated. Old Job has the best comment on Jason's shrewdness:

"You's too smart fer me. Aint a man in dis town kin keep up wid
you fer smartness. You fools a man whut so smart he cant even
keep up wid hisself," he says, getting in the wagon and unwrap-
ping the reins.

"Who's that?" I says.

"Dat's Mr. Jason Compson," he says. (267)

Concerned pragmatically with the present and his own interests, Jason stayed on in the Compson house. There were
not many Compsons left in 1928. Father, Quentin, and Caddy
were long since gone. Yet Dilsey had remained—stayed to
protect and hold together the remains of the family. She
served them all. She cooked and kept house, she put up with
Mrs. Compson's complaints and Jason's abuse, she defended
the ungrateful girl, Quentin, from Jason's violence, and she
brought some affection into Benjy's circumscribed life. In the
splintered and rotting house of Compson, she was the endur-
ing rock. Only Dilsey possessed a true family tradition and a
simple faith in God; only Dilsey, on the Easter Sunday of
1928, experienced the resurrection of Christ.

Her virtues, however, do not seem to derive primarily from
her religion. That she is free from the greed, intemperance,
and despair to which Jason, Caddy, and Quentin have, respectively, fallen victim is due chiefly to her simplicity. She
is an old Negro servant who derives her life's purpose from
the servant code of the Old South. It is her living loyalty to
the dead Compsons that explains her power to endure and
serve. She is measured, as they all are, by the capacity to
love. In Faulkner's stories and novels the power to love faith-
fully and compassionately is found—if we can judge by Aunt
Mollie Beauchamp (the old Negress who raised Roth Edmonds in *Go Down, Moses*), Grandma Millard and Aunt
Jenny (*The Unvanquished* and *Sartoris*), Monk Fentry
(*Knight's Gambit*), Byron Bunch (*Light in August*), and the

idiots (*The Sound and the Fury* and *The Hamlet*)—in simple people or in old women who identify themselves with a family. Dilsey's simplicity and family identification make her immune to the malaise and materialism that afflict Faulkner's twentieth-century world. Her compassion measures her humanity.

The love that the members of the family accord Benjy determines not only their humanity but also Benjy's. That Benjy is intended as a human being, a child dependent upon the world's tenderness, has been stated by Faulkner in explaining the genesis of *The Sound and the Fury*:

> That began as a short story, it was a story without plot, of some children being sent away from the house during the grandmother's funeral. They were too young to be told what was going on and they saw things only incidentally to the childish games they were playing, which was the lugubrious matter of removing the corpse from the house, etc., and then the idea struck me to see how much more I could have got out of the idea of the blind self-centeredness of innocence, typified by children, if one of those children had been truly innocent, that is, an idiot. So the idiot was born and then I became interested in the relationship of the idiot to the world that he was in but would never be able to cope with and just where could he get the tenderness, the help, to shield him in his innocence.[19]

It seems significant that Faulkner, when asked to explain the origin of *The Sound and the Fury*, has remembered the story as starting either from the image of a little girl's stained drawers or from the theme of an idiot's innocence. Since both the innocence and the stain are central to the Quentin section, Benjy's identification with innocence and desired tenderness links his section closely with Quentin's. The symbolic pattern of water and fire reinforces this relationship. Water in the

---

[19] *Faulkner at Nagano*, pp.103-104.

Quentin section was associated chiefly with woman and death. Benjy reacted to water too: he generally cried when Luster brought him to the branch, possibly because he associated it with the lost Caddy. The opposing symbol is fire. On the last day of his life Quentin kept thinking that if only Caddy and he could become a clean flame, the fires of hell would burn away the sins of the earth and unite brother and sister again as in their childhood. Fire played an important part in Benjy's life too. The bright flickering flames were like the "smooth, bright shapes" (94) that Benjy saw in the darkness as he lay with Caddy before falling asleep. Firelight hushed his crying and brought him peace, though it also burned him when he tried to seize it. Flowers, such as the jimson weeds he cherished and the narcissus he clutched, brought him peace too, though the flowers could be easily broken. Even his eyes were "the pale sweet blue of cornflowers" (290).[20] Fire and flowers in this context suggest a precarious peace associated with innocence and "uncorrupted" love.

Such was Benjy's love of Caddy; it was woven deeply into the fabric of his life. When he smelled the scent of perfume or of sex upon Caddy, he bellowed in protest and stirred her to temporary shame. When she was free from the scent of sex she smelled like trees to him. Still, in Benjy's innocent and timeless world, Caddy was always the smell of trees, love was always love, and she had never become a bitch. In reality the cedar trees by the hammock swing overlooked Caddy's (and later her daughter's) nightly adventures in sex,

---

[20] In an early story entitled "The Kingdom of God" (1925) Faulkner wrote of an idiot whose fist clutched a narcissus and whose "eyes were clear and blue as cornflowers"; as long as the idiot had his flower, he enjoyed the peace of the kingdom of God. See *William Faulkner: New Orleans Sketches* (New Brunswick, N.J., Rutgers University Press, 1958), pp.113-119.

and it was by a tree that her daughter descended to her young men. That was the world's reality. It was the world's reality, whether right or wrong, that decided Caddy would no longer sleep with Benjy when he became thirteen, that castrated Benjy, and that prosecuted Quentin for molesting the little Italian girl. This is why Benjy's section comes first: he represents the innocence and love that Quentin and Caddy had to forsake. Benjy never lost his childhood, but that world vanished forever for Quentin, except in his anguished memory and desire.

This theme is enriched and heightened in the last section. The major part of this section is focused on Dilsey and traces the events of Easter Sunday from dawn through the early afternoon. In the early morning the scene is set in the Compson house, but toward late morning and noon the action shifts from the church to the Mottstown road, from Dilsey to Jason. However, Faulkner does not turn his focus on Jason until he has completed his portrayal of the Easter scene in the Negro church; then he moves time back an hour or two and follows Jason from late morning through early afternoon. The structure and symbolism of this section create a counterpoint between Dilsey and Jason. The symbolism of the sun, of light, is rather important to the story. In the Compson house time was measured by the clock—"the dry pulse of the decaying house" (301)—that indicated the wrong hour; outside, time was measured by the sun.

"The day dawned bleak and chill" (281). Later, after Dilsey prepared breakfast, Jason discovered his loss and Quentin's flight. Frightened by Jason's rage, "smelling" its evil, Benjy wept and wailed—"a slow bellowing sound, meaningless and sustained" (301); "it might have been all time and injustice and sorrow become vocal for an instant by a conjunction of planets" (303-304). Benjy did not hush until he

passed out of the gate. The rain had stopped and the sun
was breaking through the swiftly moving clouds, as Dilsey
and Benjy, together with Luster and Frony, made their way
to the church. The bells were ringing the people churchward.
In the church Reverend Shegog, looking small and insignifi-
cant, rose to speak to them of the Resurrection.

He was like a worn small rock whelmed by the successive waves
of his voice. With his body he seemed to feed the voice that,
succubus like, had fleshed its teeth in him. And the congregation
seemed to watch with its own eyes while the voice consumed him,
until he was nothing and they were nothing and there was not
even a voice but instead their hearts were speaking to one another
in chanting measures beyond the need for words, so that when
he came to rest against the reading desk, his monkey face lifted
and his whole attitude that of a serene, tortured crucifix that
transcended its shabbiness and insignificance . . . (310)

As the minister gave himself up to his vision of the Christ
child, his voice shed the "cold inflectionless" (309) quality
of the white man and took on a "sad timbrous quality, . . .
sinking into their hearts" (310):

"Breddren! Look at dem little chillen settin dar. Jesus wus like
dat once. He mammy suffered de glory en de pangs. Sometime
maybe she helt him at de nightfall, whilst de angels singin him to
sleep; maybe she look out de do' en see de Roman po-lice passin.
. . . Listen, breddren! I sees de day. Ma'y settin in de do' wid
Jesus on her lap, de little Jesus. Like dem chillen dar, de little
Jesus. I hears de angels singin de peaceful songs en de glory; I
sees de closin eyes; sees Mary jump up, sees de sojer face: We
gwine to kill! We gwine to kill! We gwine to kill yo little Jesus!"
(311-312)

This is a major theme of the novel: the innocent child
killed by the world. So had Quentin regarded himself in his
heart. His thoughts of the good Jesus and "the good Saint
Francis . . . that never had a sister" (96) led him, on one hand,

to seek identification with their love and martyrdom. On the other hand, these thoughts underscored for him the difference between their love and his: they could love untroubled by sex but he could not. Benjy is closer to Jesus than Quentin is; he signifies the grace of a child's love, Quentin the loss of that grace. In striving to cling to a child's heart, Quentin had been fighting against time; it was as though he were desperately building dikes around his childhood world, but the waters of life could not be walled out. Time was Quentin's misfortune.

Dilsey, as Waggoner has noted,[21] established a different relationship to time: she drew upon the past but did not deny the present. The preacher too went back to the past for his vision of "de resurrection en de light" (312). In the midst of the vision "Ben sat, rapt in his sweet blue gaze. Dilsey sat bolt upright beside, crying rigidly and quietly in the annealment and the blood of the remembered Lamb" (313). Outdoors, the noon sun was bright and high. But later when Dilsey returned to the Compson house, she found the fire out and Mrs. Compson lying still in the half-light. As in the Quentin section, the light seems to symbolize life both natural and divine. Eighteen years ago on June 2 "the long and lonely light-rays" (96) of the sun—the rays down which, Quentin thought, "you might see Jesus walking" (96)—dwindled into utter darkness for him. Only Dilsey could make the light serve the present.

While Dilsey was resurrecting Christ, Jason was furiously pursuing his niece and money. As he passed the churches on his way to Mottstown, he visualized God as his enemy:

"And damn You, too," he said, "See if You can stop me," thinking of himself, his file of soldiers with the manacled sheriff in the

---

21 Waggoner, pp.50-51.

rear, dragging Omnipotence down from His throne, if necessary; of the embattled legions of both hell and heaven through which he tore his way and put his hands at last on his fleeing niece. (322)

At the very hour that the preacher was speaking of Christ's resurrection, Jason was contemplating His destruction. The parallel between the preacher's vision of the soldiers threatening to kill Jesus and Jason's fantasy of himself leading a file of soldiers against God points up the satanic characteristics of Jason and his Easter mission. At bright noon while Dilsey sat, "crying rigidly and quietly in the annealment and the blood of the remembered Lamb," Jason was striking the little old man in Mottstown. And in the final scene of the novel Jason vented his fury on the helpless Benjy and the hapless Luster. Jason, Faulkner seems to say, represents the world's greed, violence, and hate; moreover, his rejection of woman as a source of love is tantamount to a rejection of love itself. Hence the struggle between Dilsey and Jason seems as fundamental as that between love and hate, good and evil.

Possibly because the virtues and religion of Dilsey are so simple and convincing, there is a tendency among critics to project the spiritual values of her section into Quentin's and, in the process, to distort the nature of Quentin's character. Quentin's problem is obviously different from Dilsey's. His life is essentially narcissistic, hers self-sacrificial; he broods upon ideals, she lives them; he struggles with himself, she struggles with circumstance. Quentin's problem is chiefly that of youth: he is caught in a painful transition from boyhood to manhood, in which he strives to hold on to "sacred" love and reject "sinful" desire. Southern and puritan idealism —with its emphasis on honor, its idealization of woman, and its strong sense of guilt about sex—intensifies and blurs Quentin's problem by providing an honorable rationalization of his regression. Hence obsession becomes transformed into idealism, a morbid idealism that has contributed not only to Quentin's suicide but also to the emotional substratum of the novel. Yet the novelist struggles through morbidity to a tragic view of life. Despite the novel's inward movement down into neurosis and regression, its outward thrust is toward maturity and objectivity. The conflict between these two movements —one turning inward to the self and downward to death, the other turning outward to society and life—is central to Faulkner's works. In telling the story of the break-down of the Compson family, the author is writing about the destruction of the bridge between the self and society. The author is not Quentin Compson, for Faulkner turns from the obsessive world of Quentin to render a tragic portrayal of a disintegrating family and of the changing self.

The overall design of the novel supports this point of view. Beginning with Damuddy's death in 1898 and ending with Easter Sunday in 1928, the novel is constructed around the last thirty years of Benjy's life. Each of the major characters is measured by his relationship to time and love, while Benjy serves as the constant that determines the value of the variables of this family. Since Benjy has been "three years old thirty years" (36), he represents the timeless world of childhood. Although the novel is marked by a deep sense of nostalgia, it moves on from a vanished childhood and troubled youth to the ugly reality of Jason's world, from nostalgia to irony. It moves also from "the completely closed and private world of the first section to the completely public world of the fourth,"[22] from subjectivity to objectivity. An ironic appraisal of the world's reality mixes with a romanticist's lament for a shattered ideal. Caddy's love for Benjy, which once

---

[22] Olga W. Vickery, *The Novels of William Faulkner,* p.30.

transfigured the darkness of his nights into the "smooth bright shapes" (94) of peaceful firelight, has been reduced by time to a withered, soiled slipper. But the idiot who is also "de Lawd's child" (333) still clings to his love. This idiot incarnates the human need for love. By 1928 Jason has seized the reins of the dilapidated Compson carriage; yet his viciousness is still opposed by the compassion of Dilsey. *The Sound and the Fury* is not a tale told by an idiot signifying nothing. It is a tragedy that renders suffering into life and celebrates love.

3

Sanctuary

In less than a year after Faulkner completed *The Sound and the Fury,* he was writing another novel. It was, he said, "the most horrific tale I could imagine."[1] He wrote *Sanctuary* in three weeks—that was in the summer of 1929. But because his publisher did not dare at first to publish it and because Faulkner chose later to revise it, its publication was delayed till the early part of 1931.[2] Although the revised

---

[1] Faulkner's Introduction (1932) to the Modern Library edition of *Sanctuary,* p.vi. This edition will be used for all quotations from the text.

[2] For information on the chronology of the composition and publication of Faulkner's novels of this period, see the Introduction to *Sanctuary* (Modern Library); Linton Massey, "Notes on the Unrevised Galleys of Faulkner's *Sanctuary,*" *Studies in Bibliography,* 8 (1956), 195-208; and Frederick L. Gwynn, "Faulkner's Raskolnikov," *Modern Fiction Studies,* 4 (Summer 1958), 169-172. For information on the text, see the Massey article and James B. Meriwether, "Some Notes on the Text of Faulkner's *Sanctuary,*" *Papers of the Bibliographical Society of America,* 55 (Third Quarter 1961), 192-206. On the basis of information received from Faulkner and Linton Massey, Mr. Gwynn has compiled the following table:

	Composed	Published
Soldiers' Pay	1924	25 Feb. 1926
Mosquitoes	1926	30 Apr. 1927
Sartoris	1927	31 Jan. 1929
The Sound and the Fury	1928	7 Oct. 1929
Sanctuary (first version)	1929	—
As I Lay Dying	1929	6 Oct. 1930
Sanctuary (revised version)	1930	9 Feb. 1931

version was not done till after the writing of *As I Lay Dying,*
Sanctuary belongs, in its conception and subject, after *The
Sound and the Fury.* These two novels are different but related, as though *The Sound and the Fury* were the sweet wine
and *Sanctuary* were the bitter dregs of Faulkner's creativity
of that period.

From the story of Quentin Compson and his degenerating
family, Faulkner turned to Horace Benbow and his degenerating society, from psychological introspection to sociological
drama. Faulkner's compassionate and intense involvement
with the Compson family was replaced by an apparently detached concern with the sordid and violent aspects of the
society of the late twenties. The result was a sensational naturalistic novel characterized chiefly by "surface turbulence,
brilliant surface at times."[3] Faulkner's unwillingness to penetrate beneath the surface seems related to an aversion for the
world he was creating and to his need to put distance between himself and the protagonist.

In the writing of *Sanctuary* the author, it seems, tried to
reduce his identification with the protagonist and reduce his
preoccupation with the incest theme. Linton Massey, who
has compared both the original and revised versions of *Sanctuary,* notes that in the first version Faulkner concentrated
on the incest problem of Horace Benbow but that in the second he shifted his attention to the story of Temple Drake.[4]
Although the incest theme is still part of the revised version,
its significance, as compared with its dominance of *The
Sound and the Fury,* has obviously diminished. Moreover,
Horace's attitude to incest has changed from Quentin's: Horace regarded his desire for his stepdaughter, as well as his
affection for his sister Narcissa, with open aversion. But the

---

[3] Irving Howe, *William Faulkner: A Critical Study,* p.144.

[4] Massey, loc. cit., pp.202-203.

obsession, like the honeysuckle motif, persists in the later novel and has contributed to the making of the world of *Sanctuary*.

The novel opens at the Old Frenchman place. Once a great plantation house amid fields, lawns, and gardens, it has become a gutted ruin overrun by jungle—a bootlegger's hideout. The people who inhabit the house are part of its atmosphere of desolation and degradation. In addition to Goodwin the bootlegger, there are the old man with the blind, clotted eyes —Goodwin's father; the sick, dying child who sleeps in a box so that the rats won't get at him—Goodwin's son; and the woman with the heavy brogans, faded dress, and sullen face —ex-whore and Goodwin's unwedded wife. This family signifies both the break-down of the traditional family and the urban invasion of the countryside. The backstreets of Memphis, with their crime and prostitution, extend into this remote corner of Yoknapatawpha County. The Old Frenchman place has become a jungle where the natural and familial orders have been destroyed.

Against this background is set the unnatural rape of Temple Drake. Although Temple flees like a frightened, hysterical child from the threat of rape, her slim blond legs run toward her violation. She is lure as well as victim. Hence the brutal assault by an impotent gangster upon this delicate sexuality[5] evokes little sympathy and seems, in some ways, fitting—not merely because Temple has invited the rape but because the union of a Memphis gangster and daughter of a

---

[5] Temple Drake seems to derive from the flappers of the twenties and, in particular, from the young "epicene" females—Patricia (*Mosquitoes*), Caddy (*The Sound and the Fury*), and Cecily (*Soldiers' Pay*)—that attracted and repelled Faulkner in that period. This ambivalence is seen, for example, in the characterization of Cecily. Characterized by a soft coarseness and a delicate lust, she is both fragile and wanton. The males trail her as if she were a bitch in heat.

Jackson judge seems significant of the corruption of the New South.[6] Her "my father is a judge"—which begins as a naive boast and ends as a desperate prayer that she chants against the impending rape—is an ironic commentary on her own as well as her father's hollowness. And the blind old man who calmly and dumbly presides over the rape seems the new guardian of justice and morality.

Whatever frightened innocence Temple may have possessed at the Old Frenchman place she quickly loses at Miss Reba's brothel in Memphis, as she changes into a spoiled and vicious pet. The corrupted becomes the corrupter, the virgin the nymphomaniac. In her own way she proves as destructive as Popeye: she is instrumental in killing four men, Tommy, Red, Goodwin, and even Popeye himself. Like her rapist, she knows neither truth, justice, nor morality; she shares his childlike but deadly egoism. This child-bitch is one of the primary degenerating and destructive forces in the world of *Sanctuary*.

The other destructive force is Popeye. More symbolic than real, he seems deliberately "modernistic" and unnatural. He is cold and hard like steel, weightless like aluminum, and depthless like stamped tin. Defective product of a loveless, syphilitic union, he is apart from and against nature. He spits into a spring, shrinks in terror from an owl, and shoots a harmless dog. His foil and opponent in the first part of the novel is Ruby Lamar, a woman who struggles to fulfill a natural role in an unnatural world. He symbolizes, then, in the modern world, an unnatural, destructive force that rapes

---

[6] O'Donnell's interpretation of *Sanctuary* as an allegory about the rape and corruption of Southern Womanhood (Temple) by Modernism (Popeye) seems valid. But the meaning of the novel extends beyond the limits of this interpretation. See George Marion O'Donnell, "Faulkner's Mythology," in *William Faulkner: Three Decades of Criticism*, ed. Frederick J. Hoffman and Olga W. Vickery, pp.88-89.

and murders; the men he murders represent simple compassion and sexual potency. Forced by impotence into perversion and knowing neither compassion nor morality, he personifies a vicious, mechanistic destructiveness that is ultimately suicidal.

What Temple and Popeye represent—in its combination of sexuality, impotence, and destructiveness—plagues Horace Benbow in a strange and personal way. He was running from both Belles, his stepdaughter and his wife. For Horace, Little Belle was "the delicate and urgent mammalian whisper of that curious small flesh which he had not begot and in which appeared to be vatted delicately some seething sympathy with the blossoming grape" (200); she was part "of that conspiracy between female flesh and female season" (13). She was the embodiment of temptation and the source of sin. As he stared at her photograph which he held in his hands, he saw a "face older in sin than he ever would be" (200):

the face appeared to breathe in his palms in a shallow bath of highlight, beneath the slow, smoke-like tongues of invisible honeysuckle. Almost palpable enough to be seen, the scent filled the room and the small face seemed to swoon in a voluptuous languor, blurring still more, fading, leaving upon his eyes a soft and fading aftermath of invitation and voluptuous promise and secret affirmation like a scent itself. (267-268)

Then her image blurred with that of Temple as he saw again in his imagination the rape of Temple Drake, and he vomited. He was nauseated not only by his incestuous desire for Little Belle but by his awareness that he and she were involved in an evil to which there was no solution but death. He remembered the "expression he had once seen in the eyes of a dead child, and of other dead: the cooling indignation, the shocked despair fading, leaving two empty globes in which the motionless world lurked profoundly in miniature" (266). This feeling of despair and death Horace projected onto the world, as if the world were "approaching that moment when it must decide to turn on or to remain forever still: a motionless ball in cooling space, across which a thick smell of honeysuckle writhed like cold smoke" (267).

Horace was fleeing from his stepdaughter's sexuality, but he was fleeing too from his wife's sovereignty. In the loathed image of himself carrying a box of dripping shrimps to his wife and trailed by the "small stinking spots" (19), he saw the symbol of his humiliated manhood. His defense of Goodwin and his championing of Ruby Lamar were, like his flight, part of the rebellion against the gnawing frustration and hollow propriety of his life with Belle. But his rebellion did not change his entrapment and powerlessness; in fact, a sense of defeat—almost a desire for defeat—underlay his quixotic rebellion as if he knew that the world against which he tilted with his broken lance was too much for him. It was governed by the Belles and Narcissas, exploited by the gangsters and politicians; it was cheapened by conniving and bribery, brutalized by animalism, murder, and lynching. Its power for evil was too much for Horace Benbow.

Faulkner has not found very much to oppose this evil: the ineffectual idealism of an unsuccessful lawyer, the isolated compassion of a moron, and the aborted womanliness of a reformed whore. Ruby Lamar is one of the few sympathetic characters of *Sanctuary;* but in a world where evil triumphs readily over good, her attempt to serve as mother and wife was doomed from the start. The cards are so stacked against the few decent people of this novel that it lacks drama and reality. Despite the naturalistic details, there is a thinness to Faulkner's portrayal of life and people that prevents *Sanctuary* from being a first-rate novel. The author's aversion to the very world he was trying to create seems to have reduced his will to penetrate beneath its surface.

Although Faulkner's aversion is moral, it is also sexual; it is part of the obsessive alienation from sex which influenced Faulkner's early works.[7] In *Sanctuary* sexual revulsion underlies sexual violence. It may not be too farfetched to see in Popeye and Temple an extreme representation of what Horace saw in himself and Little Belle. Mrs. Vickery has noted "startling similarities" between Horace and Popeye: both men are painfully excluded from the sexual experiments of Temple and Little Belle; "both are conscious of their isolation and attempt to break out of it, the one through violence, the other through fantasy and hallucination which are themselves a form of violence. Popeye's brutal act fuses with Horace's thoughts and culminates in the nightmare vision of the rape of a composite Temple-Little Belle."[8] The psychological parallels between Popeye and Horace suggest that Dr. Kubie's observation that *Sanctuary* is obsessively concerned with the fears and problems of psychosexual impotence may be valid. Dr. Kubie has pointed out that in this novel "every 'respectable' man is in one way or another crippled, impotent or silly. Only the Negro who is hung, and the moonshiner who is burned alive, and Red, the dance-hall boy who is shot,

---

[7] Almost all the protagonists of these works—such as Mrs. Powers (*Soldiers' Pay*), Quentin Compson, Horace Benbow (*Sanctuary*), Addie Bundren, and the youthful Joe Christmas—felt compelled to reject sexuality. Mrs. Powers, for example, remembered her short-lived marriage as a burglarous breaking into her physical privacy. She deplored the love offered by her husband, rejected the love offered by her lover (Joe Gilligan), and married a dying aviator incapable of offering love. Addie Bundren regarded "love" as a violation of her aloneness. This psychological pattern figures still more prominently in the lives of the male protagonists.

[8] Olga W. Vickery, *The Novels of William Faulkner*, p.110.

are potent. This is true not only of the major figures such as Popeye and Benbow, but also of such minor figures as Cla'ence Snopes, or the lamed district attorney, or Gowan Stevens."[9] Even the triumph of evil and weakness over goodness and strength, Dr. Kubie infers, is related to the theme of impotence.

The association of impotence with sexual revulsion is part of an obsessional pattern in *Sanctuary* and *The Sound and the Fury*. Just as Popeye and Temple seem to represent a debased version of Horace and Little Belle, so do Horace and Little Belle represent a somewhat debased version of Quentin and Caddy Compson. The increasing debasement may have been a form of psychological disengagement— probably more subconscious than conscious—on the part of the author. This may explain why Faulkner, at the same time that he exhibits "a pronounced unwillingness to breathe the foul air of Temple and Popeye,"[10] seems compelled to enter that world, as if to lacerate his sensibilities and exorcise his obsession. And this may explain why the novel, as Irving Howe has remarked, creates an "effect resembling the aggravation of a wound rather than the catharsis of an emotion."[11]

As Temple and Popeye are felt as more and more representative of their society, the estrangement from sex merges with a moral estrangement from society. The author seems deeply cut off from the society he was trying to portray and, as a result, has relied excessively on hostile stereotypes and caricatures. The author's animosity appears to have been stronger than the artist's need to penetrate his material; it works beneath his apparent detachment. Working beneath

   [9] Lawrence S. Kubie, "William Faulkner's *Sanctuary*: An Analysis," *Saturday Review of Literature*, 11 (Oct. 20, 1934), 218, 224-226.
   [10] Howe, p.144.
   [11] Ibid.

the detachment too is a sense of futility and despair which even the burlesque comedy of the drunken funeral celebration and of the yokels in the brothel does not disperse. In *Sanctuary* the feeling of malaise is justified by the degeneracy of the society. By shifting the burden of blame from the individual to his world, the author himself seems to have benefited and the novel to have suffered. But now Faulkner was free—as he would demonstrate in *As I Lay Dying*—to write about human beings.

4

As I Lay Dying

There is a pattern to be traced in the changing character of Faulkner's sick heroes of the 1929-1930 period. The vague guilt and despair of Bayard Sartoris evolved into the specific obsession of Quentin Compson and then into the futility of Horace Benbow (*Sanctuary*). That Horace's sense of frustration is not as extreme as Bayard's or Quentin's—Horace did not commit suicide and did make an attempt to struggle against his society—suggests some lessening of the malaise. Yet all three novels—*Sartoris, The Sound and the Fury,* and *Sanctuary*—are dominated by the feeling of alienation. These three novels reflect a period of self-absorption, comparable in a sense to the period in Hawthorne's life (1825-1837) when, secluding himself in his "dismal chamber," this puritan artist of another century and another corner of America turned his mind's eye inward. For both artists the period of self-absorption seems to have been fundamental in the creation of an inner and tragic vision, but the escape from the prison of self seems to have been necessary too for their full development as artists.

For Faulkner the turning point was *As I Lay Dying*. In this novel Faulkner turned from the isolated hero to people. The simple countryfolk, the Tulls and Armstids and Bundrens, provide not only relief from the feeling of alienation but also a sense of community. *As I Lay Dying* is a comic novel rooted in the earth and countryfolk and lighted by a new faith in humanity. It marks a radical departure from *Sanctuary*, for it moves from symbols of evil to human beings, from the outlook of a cold repelled reporter to an artist who had come home. Faulkner was with his own people. No matter how comic and grotesque they might seem, they were regarded with sympathy and respect. Irving Howe has aptly commented:

Of all Faulkner's novels, *As I Lay Dying* is the warmest, the kindliest and most affectionate. . . . In no other work is he so receptive to people, so ready to take and love them, to hear them out and record their turns of idiom, their melodies of speech. . . . it shines with virtues distinctly its own: a superb sympathy for the lowly and incoherent. . . . Look—he seems to be saying—look at the capacity for suffering and dignity which human beings have, even the most absurdly wretched of them![1]

As I Lay Dying, Faulkner has said, was written "in six weeks, without changing a word."[2] Although the novel was revised,[3] it was apparently written with ease and a sense of creative power. Such a ready flow of creativity might suggest that the novel is less complex than other Faulkner works such as *The Sound and the Fury*. Certainly its language and plot are simpler, the characters less tortured and complicated, and the symbols less broodingly and consciously developed. Yet behind the simplicity there is a complexity that derives from a multiple point of view, an ambiguity of theme and symbolism, and a richly suggestive treatment of character

---

[1] Irving Howe, *William Faulkner: A Critical Study*, p.141.

[2] Introduction to *Sanctuary* (Modern Library), p.vii.

[3] James B. Meriwether, "The Literary Career of William Faulkner: Catalogue of an Exhibition," *The Princeton University Library Chronicle*, XXI (Spring 1960), p.128.

and event. The indeterminate point of view—there is no Dilsey to serve as an ethical norm—and the general lack of ex-
plicitness on the part of the author have led to diverse and
conjectural interpretations on the part of the critics.[4] This
interpretation is inevitably conjectural too, for any attempt
to explore the meaning of As I Lay Dying demands an imaginative as well as a close reading of the text.

It may be useful not only to examine the text of As I Lay
Dying closely—the themes, tensions, characters, and symbols
—but also to examine it in the context in which it was written,
particularly in its relationship to The Sound and the Fury.
Although the characters of the two novels are obviously
different, both works are concerned with the clashes within
a family and both make use of a funeral—Damuddy's or
Addie's—to initiate the story's action and to reveal the chil-

---

[4] The germinal article on As I Lay Dying is Mrs. Vickery's; it regards the novel chiefly as a study of family tension. This view has won
general acceptance and seems the soundest point of departure for a
study of this novel. However, each critic's interpretation of the major
theme or themes of As I Lay Dying tends to vary. For example, Robert
Penn Warren stresses "the heroic effort of the Bundren family to fulfill
the promise to the dead mother," Irving Howe the author's sympathetic
rendering of the inner history of the Bundren family, William Van
O'Connor the obligation to be involved, Richard Chase the quest for
identity and the discovery of kinship, Edward Wasiolek the bitterness
of man's life, William J. Handy the inner world of man and the need
for love, Frederick J. Hoffman the tension between the brothers Darl
and Jewel, and Hyatt H. Waggoner the religious vision of As I Lay
Dying. See Olga W. Vickery, The Novels of William Faulkner, pp.50-65
(or William Faulkner: Three Decades of Criticism, pp.232-247);
Robert Penn Warren, "William Faulkner," Three Decades of Criticism,
pp.119-120; Irving Howe, op. cit., pp.127-142; William Van O'Connor,
The Tangled Fire of William Faulkner, pp.45-54; Richard Chase, The
American Novel and Its Tradition, pp.206-210; Edward Wasiolek,
"As I Lay Dying: Distortion in the Slow Eddy of Current Opinion,"
Critique, 3 (Spring-Fall 1959), 15-23; William J. Handy, "As I Lay
Dying: Faulkner's Inner Reporter," Kenyon Review, 21 (Summer
1959), 437-451; Frederick J. Hoffman, William Faulkner (New York,
Twayne, 1961), pp.60-65; and Hyatt H. Waggoner, William Faulkner:
From Jefferson to the World, pp.62-87.

dren's character. Both employ the stream-of-consciousness technique, but in *As I Lay Dying* it seems more of a device than an integral function of the novel. In fact, the fifteen streams of consciousness in *As I Lay Dying* give it the appearance of being more complex than *The Sound and the Fury*. But this is not so. The action, except for a handful of flashbacks, moves in a straightforward line, while the constant shift in the interior monologues creates an effect of slow progression. The backbone of the story is the journey; the climaxes are the river and the fire scenes. Time does not double back and forth, nor does the author make much use of the tortuous recall of the past, as he did in *The Sound and the Fury*. The flashbacks are placed immediately before and after the river and fire scenes to heighten the effect and deepen the meaning of these events. The writing, especially in these scenes, is highly symbolic, yet simple and swift in movement.

The interior monologues serve three purposes: to carry the action forward, to reveal the secret selves of the characters, and to comment on the action and the other characters.[5] Nineteen of the fifty-nine monologues belong to Darl. He dominates the telling of the story. In effect its chief narrator, he narrates the crucial events and shines a light into the nature of the other characters. At times he seems clairvoyant, unrealistically so, in his ability to describe a scene from which he is absent, as on the occasion of Addie's death. Even more striking is his power to see into the secret fears and hopes of the others, to sense their concealed and subconscious feelings, thoughts, and motives. Combined with his intuitive sensitivity is a poetic articulateness. The language of *As I*

---

[5] Olga W. Vickery was the first to develop this idea; see *The Novels of William Faulkner,* pp.50-51, or her essay in *William Faulkner: Three Decades of Criticism,* pp.232-234.

Lay Dying is most moving and sensitive when Darl is reflect-
ing or observing. The imagery often has the simple, limpid
poetry of the fine passages of Twain's *Life on the Mississippi*
and *Huckleberry Finn*. There are many memorable passages:

I used to lie on the pallet in the hall, waiting until I could hear
them all asleep, so I could get up and go back to the bucket. It
would be black, the shelf black, the still surface of the water a
round orifice in nothingness, where before I stirred it awake
with the dipper I could see maybe a star or two in the bucket,
and maybe in the dipper a star or two before I drank. (344)[6]

He spits with decorous and deliberate precision into the pocked
dust below the porch. (348)

Back running, tunnelled between the two sets of bobbing mule
ears, the road vanishes beneath the wagon as though it were a
ribbon and the front axle were a spool. (365)

All her failing life appears to drain into her eyes. (371)

He looks up at the gaunt face framed by the window in the twilight. It is a composite picture of all time since he was a
child. (371)

Below the sky sheet-lightning slumbers lightly; against it the
trees, motionless, are ruffled out to the last twig, swollen, increased as though quick with young. (392)

It begins to rain. The first harsh, sparse, swift drops rush through
the leaves and across the ground in a long sigh, as though of
relief from intolerable suspense. They are big as buckshot, warm
as though fired from a gun; they sweep across the lantern in a
vicious hissing. (392)

And it is Darl who movingly describes the making of the coffin and the death of Addie, Darl who excitingly re-creates the
river and fire scenes, Darl who makes Jewel and the horse

---

[6] The Modern Library edition is used for all quotations from *As I
Lay Dying*.

come powerfully alive for us, and Darl who poignantly portrays his own ride to the Jackson asylum. No wonder reader
and author tend to identify with Darl; Darl is poetic madness, the isolated self, the son who cannot find his identity.

Addie too felt isolated. Unable in her youth to break down
the wall of her pride and ego, she—like other proud and
lonely orphans in Faulkner's works—could not establish a
relationship with others. She did not respond unless the
relationship involved pain; hence as a schoolteacher she related herself to the pupils only when she whipped them.
Nor was her feeling of estrangement and inner rebellion
eradicated by her marriage. Sexual union she tolerated reluctantly as though it were a violation of the aloneness of her
life. The birth of a child was an invasion of this aloneness,
yet her sense of violation healed after Cash's birth. Then
Anse's "love" tricked her again, and Darl was born. Her resentment turned against the child, and Darl felt the rejection
keenly. Addie had remained "a lonely woman, lonely with
her pride" (353).

Addie's estrangement from her society is evidenced in her
loss of faith in the world's "high dead words" (467): "God's
love and His beauty and His sin" (466) and the other words
"that are just the gaps in peoples' lacks, coming down like
the cries of geese out of the wild darkness in the old terrible
nights, fumbling at the deeds like orphans to whom are
pointed out in a crowd two faces and told, That is your father,
your mother" (466). Addie could not believe in a religion or
morality based on words, not deeds, "because people to whom
sin is just a matter of words, to them salvation is just words
too" (468). Out of her estrangement she embraced the sin
of adultery, as though, in Byronic fashion, she were seeking
reality through sin and were making her gesture of defiance
and rebellion. She committed adultery with the Reverend

Whitfield to make "the sin more utter and terrible" (466). It was her way of proclaiming her selfhood and of voicing her nihilistic scorn for the spurious and unfelt quality of the others' lives. Let Anse and the others live by their dead words, but Addie Bundren silently insisted, " 'I would be I' " (465).[7]

---

[7] The reasons for Addie's alienation and disillusionment are not explained in the novel. They may be related to the author's situation at the time of the writing of *As I Lay Dying*. In the summer of 1929 Faulkner, at the age of thirty-one, was still regarded by his fellow townsmen as a failure and poseur. Five years of writing novels had produced three financial failures and apparently another one in prospect. To earn a living—he had got married that summer—he was shoveling coal in a power plant. There in the middle hours of the night shift when work was slack he composed *As I Lay Dying*.

Such a situation may well have been galling for a descendant of one of the leading families of north Mississippi. Faulkner's great-grandfather, Colonel William Falkner, had been a military and political leader in the Civil War and Reconstruction eras. Lawyer, landowner, Confederate soldier, railroad builder, and even a popular novelist, the Colonel had been a man of action, even of violence. In contrast, his great-grandson was considered an unsuccessful writer who received no acceptance and served no purpose in his society. A similar kind of contrast exists between the old and new generations of the South that Faulkner portrayed in *Sartoris* and *The Sound and the Fury* and would later portray in *Light in August, Absalom, Absalom!* and *Go Down, Moses*. In Faulkner's works the Civil War soldiers like Colonel Sartoris, whose character was based on Colonel Falkner's, are characterized by their power of action and leadership; their twentieth-century descendants, like Quentin Compson and Horace Benbow and Bayard Sartoris (and later Gail Hightower), are characterized by their inability to relate to society and life. The men of the Old South lived by the deed; their descendants generally took refuge in words. Like Hawthorne with his haunting sense of the ancestral past, Faulkner felt keenly the difference between his ancestors' power to act and his own generation's sense of impotence. In *As I Lay Dying* Addie Bundren's challenge of the world's words may have expressed the author's defiance of the world and his self-distrust.

For information on Colonel William Falkner—there are contradictions in the accounts—see *Biographical and Historical Memoirs of Mississippi* (Chicago, Goodspeed Co., 1891), II, 713-714; Robert Cantwell, "The Faulkners: Recollections of a Gifted Family," *New World Writing* (Second Mentor Selection, 1952), 300-315; Robert Cantwell, Introduction to William C. Falkner's *The White Rose of Memphis* (New York, Coley Taylor, 1953), v-xxvii; Andrew Brown, "The First Missis-

Her distrust of the word and her respect for the deed not only characterize Addie but contribute to two major themes in the novel: the power to act and the power of love. Both themes are significantly involved with Addie and Jewel Bundren. Jewel was the child of Addie's sin and rebellion.[8] He was of her alone. He served his mother as a reminder of her sin and as a reason for living. He evoked from her a deep voiceless love, for which she almost hated herself. At his birth her "wild blood boiled away and the sound of it ceased. Then there was only the milk, warm and calm, and I lying calm in the slow silence, getting ready to clean my house" (467). To make amends to Anse, she gave him Dewey Dell

sippi Partisan Rangers, C. S. A.," *Civil War History*, I (Dec. 1955), 371-399; Maud Morrow Brown, "William C. Falkner, Man of Legends," *Georgia Review*, 10 (Winter 1956), 421-438; Donald Philip Duclos, *Son of Sorrow: The Life, Works and Influence of Colonel William C. Falkner, 1825-1889* (University of Michigan doctoral dissertation, 1961, microfilmed in 1962); and Thomas Felix Hickerson, *The Falkner Feuds* (Chapel Hill, N.C., Colonial Press, 1964).

[8] There are certain parallels between *As I Lay Dying* and *The Scarlet Letter:* the adulterous heroine; the child of sin, the mother's pearl or jewel; and the sinful minister and his problem of expiation (there is a contrast, however, between Dimmesdale and Whitfield; the former struggled to expiate his sin through suffering and confession, but the latter equated the intent with the deed and scurried to a quick refuge in words). These parallels do not necessarily point up any Hawthorne influence on Faulkner, but they do point up a similar concern about sin and moral truth. There is a significant relationship between the two authors, as critics have noted. For a more detailed comparison of *The Scarlet Letter* and *As I Lay Dying*, see Harold J. Douglas and Robert Daniel, "Faulkner and the Puritanism of the South," *Tennessee Studies in Literature*, 2 (1957), 6-10. For further study of the relationship between Faulkner and Hawthorne, see Malcolm Cowley, "Introduction to *The Portable Faulkner*," in *Three Decades of Criticism*, pp.95-96, 102, 108-109; Randall Stewart, "Hawthorne and Faulkner," *College English*, 17 (Feb. 1956), 258-262; Randall Stewart, "The Vision of Evil in Hawthorne and Faulkner," in *The Tragic Vision and the Christian Faith*, ed. Nathan A. Scott, Jr. (New York, Association Press, 1957), pp.238-263; and William Van O'Connor, "Hawthorne and Faulkner: Some Common Ground," *Virginia Quarterly Review*, 33 (Winter 1957), 105-123.

and Vardaman; then he had three children to call his own. Now she was ready to die, for she had come to feel the terrible truth of her father's belief "that the reason for living was to get ready to stay dead a long time" (461). Yet even in the face of this despairing outlook she had sustained herself by her "duty to the alive" (466) and had served them as mother.

She lay dying now, dying as she had lived—alone in spirit. The little life that remained to her seemed a tired light bending toward extinction.[9] As she labored to raise herself to call her sons, Jewel and Cash, her eyes were "like lamps blaring up just before the oil is gone" (370). Jewel had gone with Darl to deliver a load of wood; Cash was making the coffin. She lay back, and death blew out the flame in her eyes.

The death of Addie Bundren sets in motion an intense family struggle as well as a macabre funeral journey. In the picture of the family as it began the slow hot journey to Jefferson, bearing the mother's corpse in its midst, the nature and motives of each member are revealed. Cash sat composedly in the back of the wagon with his box of tools; Darl, the coffin at his feet, was laughing queerly; Dewey Dell sat alert and suspicious, her Sunday clothes wrapped secretly in a newspaper parcel; Vardaman mused wishfully and disconnectedly on the shiny red train in the Jefferson store window; Anse, humped over the reins, was thinking about the false teeth; and Jewel, wooden-faced and erect, rode on his spirited horse. Underlying and penetrating through their secret selves is the tension that divides the family. The tension, stemming

---

[9] Addie is generally associated with light, Anse with a bird—a blinking owl or humped buzzard—whose associations with night and death underscore the incongruity of the union of these two people. Yet Anse seems exempt from moral condemnation, so comically and affectionately is he treated by his creator.

from the mother, is concentrated in the relationship between the two brothers, Darl and Jewel.

What Jewel represents is bound up with his horse. As the wagon prepared to move into the yellow turbulent water of the flooded stream, Darl remembered how the horse first came into Jewel's life. It happened in the summer when Jewel was fifteen. He could not stay awake; he slept even when he was milking, hoeing, or eating. Somehow Addie got his chores done for him, but he lost flesh and stumbled in sleep all day long. Anxiously Addie would sit "in the dark by Jewel ... she had to love him" (429). This situation continued through the summer and fall, until one November morning Jewel galloped up to the family on a prancing spotted horse. It was the horse he had earned by working nights for five months, clearing forty acres of Quick's new ground. " 'Jewel,' ma said, looking at him. 'I'll give—I'll give—give——' Then she began to cry. She cried hard, not hiding her face, standing there in her faded wrapper, looking at him and him on the horse, looking down at her, his face growing cold and a little sick looking until he looked away quick and Cash came and touched her" (434). She wept out of relief and concern over her son; she wept because she knew that her son had turned from his mother to love another.

The love between Addie and Jewel was the central fact of Addie Bundren's life. The children born before and after Jewel, with the possible exception of Cash, figured much less in her emotional life. On her deathbed it was Jewel she wanted first, then Cash. Her love for Jewel derived partly from the burden he placed upon her: the sinful conception, the hard birth, his tantrums and devilments, and the deceit she practised for his sake. In the change from the fury of her "wild blood" to the new serenity, she had become part of him and he of her. Jewel's love for his mother was equally intense, though less articulate. He expressed his love, in a sense, by cursing and caressing his horse. The horse, as Mrs. Vickery has noted,[10] is a substitute for the mother, and the savage affection he gave it resembles the pattern of petting and whipping his mother gave him.

The horse in *As I Lay Dying* symbolizes woman and masculine power. In other works Faulkner has associated the mounted figures of Hightower's grandfather, Colonel Sartoris, and Colonel Sutpen with the doers and soldiers of the world. Faulkner's image of the charging horse signifies the power of action: in *Light in August* there is the haunting image of Hightower's grandfather charging on a horse to a flaming Union depot, and in an early autobiographical piece entitled "Carcassonne" a young poet broods on the image of a riderless Norman steed as it charges in pride and fury, though severed in half by a Saracen blade. Identifying with the charging horse, the poet dreams:

I want to perform something bold and tragical and austere he repeated, shaping the soundless words in the pattering silence *me on a buckskin pony with eyes like blue electricity and a mane like tangled fire, galloping up the hill and right off into the high heaven of the world.*[11]

In this context horse and fire symbolize a driving, masculine force toward which the poet aspires in his dream of power; in actuality the force has been severed. But in *As I Lay Dying* the horse and fire associated with Jewel signify an unsevered masculinity. In the centaur-like image of Jewel and his horse, man and animal are fleshed into a fiery union of power:

He moves. Moving that quick his coat, bunching, tongues swirl-

---

[10] Olga W. Vickery, *The Novels of William Faulkner*, pp.59 and 61.
[11] *Collected Stories of William Faulkner* (New York, Random House, 1950), p.899; this story was originally published in *These 13*.

ing like so many flames. With tossing mane and tail and rolling eye the horse makes another short curveting rush and stops again, feet bunched, watching Jewel. Jewel walks steadily toward him, his hands at his sides. Save for Jewel's legs they are like two figures carved for a tableau savage in the sun.

When Jewel can almost touch him, the horse stands on his hind legs and slashes down at Jewel. Then Jewel is enclosed by a glittering maze of hooves as by an illusion of wings; among them, beneath the upreared chest, he moves with the flashing limberness of a snake. For an instant before the jerk comes on to his arms he sees his whole body earth-free, horizontal, whipping snake-limber, until he finds the horse's nostrils and touches earth again. Then they are rigid, motionless, terrific, the horse back-thrust on stiffened, quivering legs, with lowered head; Jewel with dug heels, shutting off the horse's wind with one hand, with the other patting the horse's neck in short strokes myriad and caressing, cursing the horse with obscene ferocity.

They stand in rigid terrific hiatus, the horse trembling and groaning. Then Jewel is on the horse's back. He flows upward in a stooping swirl like the lash of a whip, his body in mid-air shaped to the horse. (345-346)

Although closely associated with the horse, Jewel is part of another symbolic pattern. He is the first character to enter the novel: "his pale eyes like wood set into his wooden face, he crosses the floor in four strides with the rigid gravity of a cigar-store Indian" (339). This patterned description of Jewel's tall lean figure and pale eyes staring out of a high-colored wooden face recurs about a dozen times. In the novel there are over fifty references to eyes and over twenty-five to wood. Most of the family, with the exception of the owlish Anse, communicate with their eyes rather than words. Addie's eyes push Doc Peabody out of her room, Darl's eyes tell Dewey Dell he knows her secret, Dewey Dell's eyes plead fiercely with the druggists for help, and in a final farcical flourish a pop-eyed woman becomes the second Mrs. Bundren. Still it is Jewel with whom references to eyes and wood are most frequently associated. Despite the fury that constantly grips him, he speaks little throughout the story, and his eyes flare whitely as he breaks into a violent act or curse. His eyes register intense but inarticulate emotion. He has the inarticulateness of a primitive who takes no refuge in words "fumbling at the deeds like orphans" (466). Jewel is no orphan; he is Addie's son. Addie's distrust of words is curiously embodied in Jewel, so that his emotion leaps over "dead words" and flames into the living deed. In his insulation from the enervating effect of words and in his power to act, Jewel stands, like the tall convict in *The Wild Palms,* for the strength of simplicity. The woodenness of Jewel reinforces this inarticulateness and suggests a rigidity of response which is the product of his unconsidered rush into action. But probably the most important function of Jewel's woodenness is to associate him with Addie. When Addie lay on her deathbed, her hands were two gnarled and unwashed roots (347) and her body "no more than a bundle of rotten sticks" (369). After death her "pole-thin body" (407) became part of the "bleeding plank" (385) of the coffin. The coffin that "slumbered lightly alive, waiting to come awake" (395) would have to be borne through water and fire before Addie Bundren was to find salvation.

In one sense, *As I Lay Dying* is a comic novel that combines a humorous portrayal of countryfolk with the grotesque violence of the tall tale; in another sense, it is a fable about Addie's quest for salvation. The crossing of the river was attended by signs of disaster as if Cora Tull were right, after all, in her insistence that the carting of Addie's corpse to Jefferson was a flouting of God's will. The description of the actual disaster seems to bear out her judgment: a bearded log rose suddenly out of the water, "stood for an instant upright upon that surging and heaving desolation like Christ"

(445), and swiftly bore down upon the helpless wagon. It lunged and struck at the wagon. "Soon as the wagon got tilted good, to where the current could finish it, the log went on. It headed around the wagon and went on good as a swimming man could have done. It was like it had been sent there to do a job and done it and went on" (449). Cora Tull said it was the hand of God (448). Yet the self-righteous and unperceptive Cora may not be as reliable a witness for God as Addie Bundren. Cora had condemned Addie as "a poor blind woman" who "had closed her heart to God and set that selfish mortal boy [Jewel] in His place" (461); but Addie had replied, " 'He is my cross and he will be my salvation. He will save me from the water and from the fire. Even though I have laid down my life, he will save me' " (460). If Addie's prophecy is correct, the journey that may have begun as a flouting of God's will has been transfigured into the journey to salvation. The proof lies in the testing of the chosen son.

As I Lay Dying is a fable not only about Addie's quest for salvation but about the testing of three sons by the ordeals of water and fire. Their crossing of the flooded river with the mother's corpse is the first test. When disaster, in the shape of the log, threatened the sons and their mother, Darl abandoned the wagon, Cash struggled to stay with the coffin as the river overpowered him, and Jewel fought his horse back to the coffin. Darl came out of the water with empty hands, Cash with the horse (the substitute for the mother), and Jewel with the prize—the coffin. The rescue of the coffin may be interpreted in two ways: it signifies the living mother that Jewel saves, and it signifies the love that Jewel retains.[12]

---

[12] Mrs. Vickery has observed that "the circumstances of the birth of her children establish the level of their awareness of Addie and the mode of their response to and participation in her burial" (*The Novels of William Faulkner*, p.55). The river scene is a reminder of

Cash and Jewel sacrificed what they loved: Cash his tools, Jewel his horse. Cash's sacrifice was returned, but Jewel's was accepted. Darl had nothing to sacrifice.

The clash between Darl and Jewel is closely related to the question of Addie's love. Immediately prior to the fire scene the air becomes electric with the tension between them:

> "Your mother was a horse, but who was your father, Jewel?"
> "You goddamn lying son of a bitch."
> "Don't call me that," I say.
> "You goddamn lying son of a bitch."
> "Don't you call me that, Jewel."
>
> .   .   .   .
>
> *Jewel, I say, Who was your father, Jewel?*
> *Goddamn you. Goddamn you.* (494-495)

Darl is the loveless child striking at the beloved son; Jewel has the love that gives him his identity and possibly his power. Out of his sense of emptiness and involuntary envy, Darl set fire to the Gillespie barn. Although he may have felt that the carting of Addie's decaying corpse had become an offense against her and society, his primary motive seems to have been the need to burn Addie out of Jewel's life and to hurt Jewel.

The tension continues through the violent action of the fire scene, which is narrated in the historical present by Darl. In the midst of the burning barn Darl with strange detachment observes the heroic action of Jewel:

He [Jewel] pauses at the coffin, stooping, looking at me, his

---

the birth of the three sons; in fact, the action of the scene stops in one place as Darl and Cash recall the birth of Jewel. There are some vague parallels between the river and the womb: for example, the way in which Cash is delivered from the water may suggest a kind of rebirth; certainly Cash, as critics have noted, undergoes a moral rebirth as a result of his suffering.

face furious. Overhead the flames sound like thunder; across us rushes a cool draught: there is no heat in it at all yet, and a hand-fall of chaff lifts suddenly and sucks swiftly along the stalls where a horse is screaming. "Quick," I say; "the horses."

He glares a moment longer at me, then at the roof overhead, then he leaps toward the stall where the horse screams. It plunges and kicks, the sound of the crashing blows sucking up into the sound of the flames. (498)

After rescuing the animals, Jewel returns to save Addie. Darl tries to stop him, but Jewel breaks away from him and Gillespie and re-enters the fire.

. . . he up-ends the coffin and slides it single-handed from the saw-horses. It looms unbelievably tall, hiding him: I would not have believed that Addie Bundren would have needed that much room to lie comfortable in; for another instant it stands upright while the sparks rain on it in scattering bursts as though they engendered other sparks from the contact. Then it topples for-ward, gaining momentum, revealing Jewel and the sparks raining on him too in engendering gusts, so that he appears to be enclosed in a thin nimbus of fire. Without stopping it overends and rears again, pauses, then crashes slowly forward and through the cur-tain. This time Jewel is riding upon it, clinging to it, until it crashes down and flings him forward and clear and Mack leaps forward into a thin smell of scorching meat and slaps at the widening crimson-edged holes that bloom like flowers in his undershirt. (501)

Jewel seems to ride the coffin out of a fiery hell into a glorious peace.

The scene is invested with a sense of triumph and libera-tion. Darl has been replaced by Jewel as the novel's pro-tagonist, words by action; and Addie, lonely rebel and stoic mother, has found her final justification in her bastard son. It is a triumph whose significance is felt all the more keenly if one compares the novel with *The Sound and the Fury*. *The Sound and the Fury* tells of the doomed and morbid love of

brother and sister; *As I Lay Dying* tells of the victorious love
of mother and son. Addie and Jewel Bundren have replaced
Caddy and Quentin Compson. Unable to resolve the dilemma
of his love, the idealistic and introverted Quentin drowned
himself; borne by the power of his love, the wordless and
uncomplicated Jewel explodes into the fiery deed. Jewel does
"not love in word, neither in tongue; but in deed and truth"
(1 John 3:18). In *As I Lay Dying* love is a voiceless, inspirit-
ing force that bears the son out of water and fire and converts
emotion into the living deed. To this love Faulkner has as-
signed the power of salvation. Now Addie can say, "I have
laid down my life that I might take it again."

As I Lay Dying was Faulkner's novel of liberation. He
broke out of the prison of self to discover his people and the
power of love. He found in the countryfolk of Yoknapatawpha a basis for faith in mankind. When he fused anguish
with comedy and discovered in love the power to act, he
struck a new note of affirmation. He found the style that was
right for his subject; the language of this novel, in its simplicity and naturalness and poetry, is reminiscent of Twain
at his best. He found too themes appealing to his heart but
undominated by obsession. This fable of mother and sons
is a minor masterpiece.

acters; ultimately he determines what the characters and the novel mean. Since the meaning of *Light in August* is bound up with the meaning of Joe Christmas, this study might well begin with the beginning of his life.

The central significance of Joe Christmas' life was established before he was born. Doc Hines, his grandfather, had shot his father and brought about his mother's death too. As a result, Joe was born an orphan into a world that wanted no part of him. His grandfather hated him not only as the "nigger bastard of bitchery" but as "the Lord God's abomination." Even his well-meaning grandmother wondered whether he was the child of the Lord or the spawn of the devil. The cage of hatred and rejection into which the child had been thrust at birth remained unbroken through his five years at the Memphis orphanage. The father and mother he had there were the janitor and the dietitian; they watched over him with insane hatred. The child's alienation was further deepened by his suspicion that he was part Negro. Finally Simon McEachern's entrance into his life was to complete the shaping of a character that had been doomed from birth.

At their first meeting McEachern's voice, like the heavy rapping of a judge's hammer, struck at the child: " 'Christmas. A heathenish name. Sacrilege. I will change that.... From now on his name will be McEachern.... He will eat my bread and he will observe my religion' " (126-127). In the years that followed, McEachern strove in the name of God to beat his religion into the unflinching, resisting boy. He instructed him that the Lord was an angry, vengeful God, that man was conceived in sin and bound in penance to lifelong toil, that the virtues the Lord demanded were work and fear of God, and that the sins He abominated were sloth and lechery. The boy resisted the hard Calvinism of the man and the "soft kindness" (147) of the man's wife. He

5

Light in August

The community, Cleanth Brooks has said, is everywhere in *Light in August* (1932). "It expresses itself through Mrs. Armstid emptying her china bank and knotting the coins into a sack for Lena; through the sheriff kicking the ineffectual bloodhounds or ordering the thrill-seekers away from his examination of the Negro witness; through the second-hand furniture dealer who relates the closing episode of the novel; and through a dozen other minor or anonymous characters."[1] Yet no matter how strong Faulkner's sense of the community may be in *Light in August,* his awareness of the individual is still more intense. Many commentators have remarked on the extreme isolation that characterizes Joanna Burden, Gail Hightower, and Joe Christmas; Kazin, for example, has described Joe Christmas as "the most solitary character in American fiction," "the ultimate personification of modern loneliness."[2] The theme of the divided and alienated self, a theme which has dominated the novels of Faulkner's great creative period that began in the late twenties and

[1] Cleanth Brooks, *William Faulkner: The Yoknapatawpha Country* (New Haven, Yale University, 1963), p.53.
[2] Alfred Kazin, "The Stillness of *Light in August,*" in *William Faulkner: Three Decades of Criticism,* pp.253, 248.

ended in the early thirties, continues to figure prominently in this, the last novel of that period. However, the author's growing social awareness made his portrayal of the isolated individual in *Light in August* more controlled and mature. He saw him as a creature both acting and acted upon, as an organic part of human society. Although Faulkner was becoming more sympathetically aware of the Southern community, he was still more strongly concerned with the individual who could not relate to his society and hence could not establish his human identity. There, Faulkner said, is "the tragic, central idea of the story," "the most tragic condition a man could find himself in—not to know what he is and to know that he will never know."[3] Joe Christmas incarnates this condition, and *Light in August* is his story.

The novel opens, however, with Lena Grove. Although Lena plays no actual part in the story of Joe Christmas, by the nature of her being she defines him as her polar opposite. She *is*, he is trying to be; she carries life, he death. She is necessary not only to provide counterpoint to the Christmas story but also to round out the vision of life that *Light in August* presents. She has the first and last word in the novel; she exists, in a sense, before and after Joe Christmas. She signifies by being.

The very first scene—as we see Lena wending her slow sure way along the country road in the "hot still pinewiney silence" (7)[4] of the August afternoon—sets the mood and establishes her significance. The scene has the quality of a pastoral, peaceful and benign. As she rides in the wagon, yielding herself to its slow rhythm and watching the road unwind gradually between the mule's ears, she becomes part

of the dreamy, bemused afternoon. Like the slow[...] ing sun, this country girl big with child seems [...] the scene's peace and quiet flow of time. Sh[...] with the people too, quietly and placidly inv[...] kindliness. Her month-old journey from Alaba[...] sissippi in a seemingly hopeless quest for the fa[...] unborn child has proved to be a "peaceful cor[...] with unflagging and tranquil faith and peopled[...] and nameless faces" (6). She believes the Lord [...] family together when a "chap" comes, especially t[...] Her faith is instinctive, as if she drew her sere[...] from the "tranquil and calm unreason" (16) of [...] Humorously and whimsically portrayed, this ea[...] of Yoknapatawpha embodies the still, burgeoning [...] of life itself.

But the smoke she saw darkening the sky as s[...] ward the mill outside Jefferson signals our en[...] another world—the world of Joe Christmas. He[...] interpreted variously by the critics as a Snopes [...] villain, a mixture of heroism and pathos, a social [...] victim, the existentialist anti-hero, a Christ figure, a[...] hero.[5] Whatever he may represent, he is certainly[...] center, the source of its tensions and the concern [...]

---

[3] *Faulkner in the University*, p.72.

[4] The Modern Library edition is used for all quotations from *Light in August*.

[5] See George Marion O'Donnell, "Faulkner's Mythology,[...] *Faulkner: Three Decades of Criticism*, pp.89-90; Malc[...] "Introduction to *The Portable Faulkner*," in *Three Decades*[...] p.103; Robert Penn Warren, "William Faulkner," in *Three*[...] *Criticism*, p.121; Richard Chase, *The American Novel and [...]* pp.213-214; William Van O'Connor, *The Tangled Fire [...] Faulkner*, pp.72-87; Ilse Dusoir Lind, "The Calvinistic Bur[...] *in August*," *New England Quarterly*, 30 (Sept. 1957), 307-[...] M. Slabey, "Joe Christmas, Faulkner's Marginal Man,"[...] (Fall 1960), 266-277; C. Hugh Holman, "The Unity o[...] *Light in August*," *PMLA*, 73 (March 1958), 155-166; a[...] Longley, "Joe Christmas: the Hero in the Modern Worl[...] *Decades of Criticism*, pp.265-278 .

held tight to his orphan's identity rather than be remade in another man's image. He had to resist.

The long fierce struggle between Joe Christmas and his foster father seems strangely compelled and desired, as if each achieved some kind of fulfillment from it. Its first dramatic and apparently symbolic expression occurred in the stable on the Sabbath morning when, hour after hour, McEachern whipped the boy for not learning the catechism:

When the strap fell he [Joe] did not flinch, no quiver passed over his face. He was looking straight ahead, with a rapt, calm expression like a monk in a picture. McEachern began to strike methodically, with slow and deliberate force, still without heat or anger. It would have been hard to say which face was the more rapt, more calm, more convinced. (131)

The boy's face was lifted, "his attitude one of exaltation" (131); the bearded face, like that of an Old Testament figure, was "firm as carved stone" (131). Later, after the boy recovered consciousness, "the ruthless man who had never known either pity or doubt" (133) forced him to kneel and began to pray. "He prayed for a long time, his voice droning, soporific, monotonous. He asked that he be forgiven for trespass against the Sabbath and for lifting his hand against a child, an orphan, who was dear to God" (133). He rose over the kneeling boy and lit the lamp, the flame steadying upon the wick "beneath the globe upon which the man's hand appeared now as if it had been dipped in blood. The shadows whirled and steadied. McEachern lifted something from the table beside the lamp: the catechism. He looked down at the boy: a nose, a cheek jutting, granitelike, bearded to the caverned and spectacled eyesocket. 'Take the book,' he said" (134).

If the intense stubborn struggle between the bearded puritan and his foster son, between dogmatic authority and the suffering boy has religious overtones, the explanation of C. Hugh Holman that "the stern Calvinism of Simon McEachern represents the accepted religious order of Joe's world, an equivalent of the Pharisaic order of Christ's"[6] is a likely one. Yet it does not follow, even though this Christian analogy may be implicit in the McEachern-Christmas clash, that Christian symbolism is an integral, significant part of *Light in August*. Despite the persuasive case that Holman has made for interpreting Joe Christmas as the Christ who is the suffering servant of the Book of Isaiah, most commentators do not accept the religious interpretation; and they, it seems to me, are essentially correct. Not only are many of the novel's parallels to the Christ story "nebulous, fleeting, almost wayward" and perverse,[7] as Holman has conceded, but they are limited chiefly to a certain stage or type of experience in Christmas' life—his childhood and suffering. Just as the innocent helplessness of Benjy and the suffering of Quentin Compson may have led Faulkner to identify them, consciously and unconsciously, with the image of Christ, so have those aspects of Christmas' life induced a similar response in Faulkner's creation of Joe Christmas. Yet, although Christmas may suffer, he does not serve; and even the sacrificial quality of the suffering may be questioned. Christian symbolism is used sporadically to heighten and deepen the significance of Joe Christmas, but it does not seem to be primary to the novel.

As a child Joe had been the victim of his grandfather's pathological religion of white supremacy, and as a boy he had been the victim of his foster father's narrow Calvinism. But as a youth the victim became the rebel who found ex-

---

[6] Holman, 157.
[7] Ibid.

pression for his defiance in his affair with Bobbie Allen. His rebellion reached its climax in the country dance scene where McEachern burst into the room like "the actual representative of the wrathful and retributive Throne" (178). " 'Away, Jezebel,' " McEachern thundered into the shocked silence and struck at "the face of Satan" (178) he saw in the youth he had raised and sheltered. As though enacting a fated role, he walked with "the furious and dreamlike exaltation of a martyr . . . into the descending chair which Joe swung at his head" (178). Joe rode away from the crime, "exulting perhaps at that moment as Faustus had, of having put behind now at once and for all the Shalt Not, of being free at last of honor and law. In the motion the sweet sharp sweat of the horse blew, sulphuric; the invisible wind flew past. He cried aloud, 'I have done it! I have done it! I told them I would!' " (180) The victim had turned rebel, and now like Satan the rebel had turned aggressor.

That scene marks Christmas' satanic coming of age. Having struck down the patriarchal authority of his life, he was to abandon the farm and to move in restless flight through towns and cities. He became like the homeless wanderers who used to come to Max and Mame's place: "who had just got off a train and who would be gone tomorrow and who did not have any address" (151-152). But Christmas was more alien and alone than they; for not only had he cut himself off from whatever community he possessed, but he engaged in a kind of underground war with society and himself. The question of his identity, his race, was becoming more and more urgent for him. Long ago when still a child he had claimed, " 'I aint a nigger' " (336). A Negro had answered him: " 'You are worse than that. You dont know what you are. And more than that, you wont never know. You'll live and you'll die and you wont never know,' and he says, 'God

aint no nigger,' and the nigger says, 'I reckon you ought to
know what God is, because dont nobody but God know what
you is'" (336). Now he was trying to learn what he was. He
went to live with Negroes and fought Negroes who called
him white and lived as husband with a woman black as coal.
Yet he fought the whites who called him "nigger." He provoked them all, white and black, as if he were driven to violence against the others and himself, as if he wanted them to
turn against him and break through his baleful sneer into
the unbearable aloneness. But he uttered no cry of despair
or misery and cut himself off from others. He had to reject
all bonds, because he bore within himself "the psychic
weight of multiple rejections—rejection before God, rejection
as Negro, rejection as human being."[8]

After fifteen years of wandering he was approaching the
point when the tensions of the multiple rejections were ready
to fuse and explode. It is at this point that Joanna Burden
entered his life or rather that he broke into hers. Their first
meeting was a reminder of the past he had tried to put away
and a portent of the future he could not escape. In search of
food, he climbed through the open window into her kitchen;
standing in the dark, he ate of something in a dish. Its taste
evoked his memory:

I have eaten it before, somewhere. In a minute I will memory
clicking knowing *I see I see I more than see hear I hear I see my
head bent I hear the monotonous dogmatic voice which I believe
will never cease going on and on forever and peeping I see the indomitable bullet head the clean blunt beard they too bent and I
thinking How can he be so nothungry and I smelling my mouth
and tongue weeping the hot salt of waiting my eyes tasting the
hot steam from the dish* "It's peas," he said aloud. "For sweet
Jesus. Field peas cooked with molasses." (201)

---

[8] Lind, 317.

The door opened, and a woman carrying a candle entered the room. For a moment they froze—"he with the dish, she with the candle" (202); then she said calmly and coldly, " 'If it is just food you want, you will find that' " (202). The scene is symbolic: she carried light but he wanted food. That both light and food would later be rejected is suggested by the scene's association with Christmas' memory of the praying McEachern. Nor is the association with McEachern merely coincidental. Both Joanna Burden and Simon McEachern were ruled by a rigid, fanatic faith; both developed a lacerating relationship with Christmas which was shaped largely by their antipathy and religion; and both, clean and harsh and barren, laid claim to a child they never possessed. In his union with Joanna Burden would converge the destructive tensions of Christmas' life and character: his hatred of woman, race, and religion.

He went to bed with her but he resented her. On one occasion, in the same way that he had once rejected food from Mrs. McEachern, he hurled against the wall Miss Burden's food. It was " 'woman's muck' ... *set out for the nigger*" (208). After that he went to work at the sawmill and ate in town. He hated being treated like a "nigger," and he hated woman's "soft kindness" that she used, he believed, to exploit man's weakness and to break his will and pride. Yet his antagonism stemmed from another source too: the dietitian. She was part of a past he had long since forgotten, except for vague associations of woman smells with toothpaste and vomit, and except for strange feelings of antipathy; she was part of his unconscious and irrational life. She was with him in his first attempt at sexual intercourse: he was in the shed with a Negro girl, "overcome by a terrible haste. There was something in him trying to get out, like when he had used to think of toothpaste" (137). Blindly and violently

he had repelled the girl—he did not know why. The same
abhorrence of woman's sexuality underlay his traumatic reaction when he was told about menstruation; he tried to
exorcise the horror by immersing his hands in the warm blood
of a sheep. But the same irrational abhorrence welled out
of his unconscious when Bobbie Allen told him about her
"sickness." He struck her and fled to the woods.

He reached the woods and entered, among the hard trunks, the
branch-shadowed quiet, hardfeeling, hardsmelling, invisible. In
the notseeing and the hardknowing as though in a cave he seemed
to see a diminishing row of suavely shaped urns in moonlight,
blanched. And not one was perfect. Each one was cracked and
from each crack there issued something liquid, deathcolored, and
foul. He touched a tree, leaning his propped arms against it, seeing
the ranked and moonlit urns. He vomited. (165)

The next week he dragged her to the same woods as though
he had to lay once and for all a ghost of the past.

Christmas' misogyny stems less from Bobbie Allen's final
rejection and betrayal of his love than from his early experience with the dietitian. A projection of sexual antipathy in
its deepest sense, his misogyny is one of the causes of the
murder of Joanna Burden. The Negro girl to whom he had
gone for his first sexual experience had seemed "a black well"
(137); and Joanna seemed "a sewer" (224) into which he had
fallen, "a bottomless morass" (227) into which he was being
sucked, "a swamp" (229) in which he was drowning. This
drowning-image suggests his sense of being defiled and
threatened by Joanna Burden. The image is part of an obsessive pattern that we have already noted in Faulkner's
works and that has signified for his protagonists the threat of
woman and her sexuality. In the face of this threat Horace
Benbow surrendered, Quentin Compson drowned himself,
but Joe Christmas was to murder woman though it would
cost him his life.

A second cause of Miss Burden's death was the problem of Joe's race. Taught by her father that her mission in life was to carry the burden of the "black shadow in the shape of a cross" (221), she saw the Negroes not "as people, but as a thing" (221). For her, Joe Christmas was always the Negro. Before she reached her climacteric, his race served as an aphrodisiac to her sexual desire; afterwards, his race meant the burden she had to carry. As benefactress to the black race, she offered to pay for his education at a Negro college. But when she insisted that he accept his race and live openly as a Negro, she only aggravated his tension, since he could neither accept nor reject what he did not know. Paradoxically, it was only after the murder that he felt ready to become one with his black brother. He put on the "black shoes" (289) even though he "could see himself being hunted by white men at last into the black abyss which had been waiting, try-ing, for thirty years to drown him and into which now and at last he had actually entered, bearing now upon his ankles the definite and ineradicable gauge of its upward moving" (289, 297). Both woman and race threatened, so to speak, to drown Joe Christmas.

The immediate cause inciting him to the murder of Joanna Burden, however, was her demand that he submit to God. The murder scene in certain details—the lighting of the lamp, her insistence that he kneel to God, and the stubborn strug-gle between two strong wills—recalls the scene with Mc-Eachern which took place on the Sabbath he whipped the boy for not learning the catechism. The submission she de-manded of Joe in the name of God was profoundly involved in his subconscious and unconscious mind with the religious pattern his foster father had tried to impose upon him. To submit his will to her God would be tantamount to denying his whole life of resistance; whatever identity he possessed had been made out of his alienation and resistance. They both

knew he would never yield. Still they faced one another in
weary yet indomitable antagonism, neither willing to give in,
neither willing to let the other alone. Some fatality seemed to
control and push them toward their violent end. As Christmas
waited outside in the ruined garden for the courthouse clock
to strike the right hour for her murder, "he believed with
calm paradox that he was the volitionless servant of the
fatality in which he believed that he did not believe" (244-
245). In addition to its inevitability, the murder takes place
amidst a strange calm and passiveness. While Joanna, with
the cold mad assurance of the righteous and the despair of
the damned, cocked the pistol and prepared to fire, he waited
still and detached.

> Her eyes did not waver at all. They were still as the round black
> ring of the pistol muzzle. But there was no heat in them, no fury.
> They were calm and still as all pity and all despair and all con-
> viction. But he was not watching them. He was watching the
> shadowed pistol on the wall; he was watching when the cocked
> shadow of the hammer flicked away. (247)

The scene is gripped by the despair one associates with suicide rather than murder. Although Joe Christmas killed
Joanna Burden because he felt compelled to reject woman,
God, and his race, he killed too because, like Joanna, he was
ready for death.

The murder took place sometime after a Friday midnight
in August. Seven days of flight were to go by before he would
surrender himself in Mottstown. His flight was like a nightmare that rendered a dark and painful allegory of his life.
He fled through the alternating spaces of day and night as
though he were running back and forth between the black
and white worlds that divided him and his society, running
from one to the other and rejected by both, running nowhere.
At times he seemed a spectator of his own absurd and futile

life, from which he felt cut off as if he were no longer part of existence. And there were those times when waking seemed like sleeping, and sleeping like waking, and he was caught up in a dreamlike running. He was always running; the breaks in his flight were few. There was the time when he broke into the Negro church. He mounted the pulpit, struck down the minister, cursed God, and smashed the lamps of His house as though he were struggling in a dream against the God of McEachern and Joanna Burden, as though he were cursing the maker of his own miserable life.

On the last night of his flight "a strange thing came into his mind" (293).

It was strange in the sense that he could discover neither derivation nor motivation nor explanation for it. He found that he was trying to calculate the day of the week. It was as though now and at last he had an actual urgent need to strike off the accomplished days toward some purpose, some definite day or act, without either falling short or overshooting. He entered the coma state which sleeping had now become with the need in his mind. When he waked in the dewgray of dawn, it was so crystallised that the need did not seem strange any more. (293)

It is not entirely clear what Christmas' preoccupation with the day and the place is intended to signify. There is the suggestion that he was emulating Christ in choosing Friday for the day of his "passion." But since Faulkner, just as he has contradicted himself about Joe's age,[9] has contradicted himself about the day of Joe's capture—in one part of the chapter the day is designated as Friday (298) and in another as Saturday (306)—the total effect is to blur or even to mock the Christian symbolism. Yet Joe's strange need to surrender in

---

[9] Although Faulkner leaves the reader with the impression that Christmas was thirty-three at the time of his death, he was in actual count—he was eighteen when he left McEachern, he wandered for fifteen years, and he lived with Joanna Burden for three—thirty-six.

Mottstown suggests that in returning to his origin, to the white kinsman who had first rejected him, he has been traveling all his life in a circle out of which he has never broken.

Before he was to die, he touched and affected briefly the life of another person, the Reverend Hightower. It seems significant that a defunct minister should be chosen to provide the moral and spiritual perspective of the Southern community of this novel. One might well question, in fact, how such a person, even more isolated in some ways than Joanna Burden and Christmas, could represent or lead his community. But that seems the point—he did not and he should have. After all, he had been ordained for the ministry and he came of a good Southern family. His grandfather had been a lawyer and Confederate soldier, his father a minister and doctor. But the Hightower of the twentieth century was the last of a deteriorating family, a deterioration which Faulkner seems to intend as characteristically Southern. The grandfather, "a hale, bluff, rednosed man with the moustache of a brigand chief" (412-413), had lived by a "simple adherence to a simple code" (413). He had approached life with directness and vigor: just as he had savored its pleasures simply and boldly, so had he fought for the South in which he believed. But Hightower's father was another kind. He was a cold moralist, "a man of Spartan sobriety beyond his years, as the offspring of a not overly particular servant of Chance and the bottle often is" (414). He disapproved of "his lusty and sacrilegious father" (414) and disapproved of slavery. Despite his strong abolitionist principles, "he took an active part in a partisan war and on the very side whose principles opposed his own," as if "he was two separate and complete people, one of whom dwelled by serene rules in a world where reality did not exist" (414-415). This split between principle and act, between man and society, deepened still further with the son until it became separation from life.

"Born into the autumn of his mother's and father's lives" (411), Gail Hightower grew to youth, loving darkness and fearing life. To be "sheltered from the harsh gale of living" (419), he sought refuge amid the "quiet and safe walls" (419) of the seminary. He found his most reassuring refuge, however, in the prolonged and hallucinated dream of his grandfather's heroic past. Like Emily Grierson of "A Rose for Emily" (1930), he represents the Southerner who clutches so deludedly at a dead past that life itself is denied. Both Emily and Hightower are death-in-life figures who are characterized by sickly flabbiness and foul decay and who are associated with dying light. Motionless as an "eastern idol" (78, 275 and *Collected Stories*, 123, 128), they would sit by a window at sunset and watch the light die out of the sky. At the instant that light was replaced by darkness, Hightower would relive that glorious and inglorious moment when his grandfather's cavalry, after its reckless firing of the Union depot, thundered gallantly forward and his grandfather got shot in a henhouse, stealing chickens.

. . . the consternation, the conflagration; the sky itself must have been on fire. You can see it, hear it: the shouts, the shots, the shouting of triumph and terror, the drumming hooves, the trees uprearing against that red glare as though fixed too in terror, the sharp gables of houses like the jagged edge of the exploding and ultimate earth. Now it is a close place: you can feel, hear in the darkness horses pulled short up, plunging; clashes of arms; whispers overloud, hard breathing, the voices still triumphant; behind them the rest of the troops galloping past toward the rallying bugles. (424)

Hightower's obsession with the past is complicated by the clash between his partly repressed awareness of its reality and his need to exalt the past and find sanctuary there. On one hand, the dynamic quality, as well as the sexual and masculine imagery of the scene (the fire, drumming hooves, uprearing trees, plunging horses, and hard breathing), suggests the virility and "the sheer tremendous tidal wave of desperate living" (423) that the grandfather symbolized for his twentieth-century descendant. On the other hand, the virility Hightower unconsciously desired he felt compelled to rationalize, as Quentin Compson might have done, into "that fine shape of eternal youth and virginal desire which makes heroes" (423). At the same time that Hightower represents the Southern tendency to embrace an hallucinated dream of the past and to divorce oneself from reality, he represents also a complex moral intelligence that is aware of the true situation but lacks the will to confront it. Desiring his grandfather's power to act and fleeing his father's moralism, Hightower withdrew from life to a form of death.

Faulkner's portrayal of Hightower is both critical and understanding. The author is highly critical of the dereliction of Hightower's moral responsibility to his wife, God, and his people; yet he holds out some glimmering hope of redemption for the minister who had tried to purchase immunity from life's troubles by a spurious martyrdom. It is not the physical impotence but the moral evasion that makes Hightower culpable for his wife's desertion, madness, and suicide; his disregard of his wife's well-being was a willed blindness. The same temptation to flight from moral responsibility besets him in his relation to Joe Christmas. Joe's claim on the minister is the Negro's claim on the white Southern conscience; Hightower recognizes him as "poor man, poor mankind" (87). In his last hours Joe becomes the Negro pursued by the white Southerner who has identified faith in white supremacy with loyalty to America and the South.

Although *Light in August* is principally the story of Christmas' struggle to realize human identity, it is also the story
of Hightower's struggle to realize moral responsibility. Both
are seeking in their own ways to become human. For Hightower their meeting represents the climax of his moral dilemma, for Christmas his last defiance of God. Yet when
Christmas comes running to God's minister, there is a vague
suggestion that in his last hour Joe may relent in his hatred
of God and beseech aid of "my shield, and the horn of my
salvation, my high tower[10] and my refuge, my saviour" (II
Sam. 22:3). But too much was running with Christmas—more
than thirty years of resistance and rebellion. And too long
had the minister huddled in a dead and illusionary past.
Although Hightower did make a futile attempt to protect
the Negro from his white pursuer, it was too late. Christmas
raised his "armed and manacled hands full of glare and
glitter like lightning bolts, so that he resembled a vengeful
and furious god pronouncing a doom" (406) and struck the
minister down. The South that Hightower failed to lead to
"the crucified shape of pity and love" (428) turned for its
leadership to the zealous soldier of white supremacy, Percy
Grimm. It was the South of the pistol and the knife that left
its final mark upon Joe Christmas. Still, according to Faulkner, the "peaceful and unfathomable and unbearable eyes"
(407) of the crucified Negro had, in turn, left their mark
upon the Southern conscience. Christmas died, but the shame
lived on.

As their lives had touched for one destructive instant, Joe
Christmas, Joanna Burden, and Gail Hightower struggled,

---

[10] Hightower's name seems an ironic commentary on his physical
and spiritual manhood. Most of the names in *Light in August* comment,
either ironically or not, on the nature of the character: Joe Christmas,
Eupheus Hines, Percy Grimm, Burden, Simon, Bobbie Allen, Lena
Grove, and Byron.

each in his own way, to become human and to break out of
darkness into light. Yet their lives remained overshadowed
by darkness and they themselves remained captives of death.
The light in the novel is provided, of course, by Byron Bunch
and Lena Grove. In the contrasting pattern of light against
darkness and of life against death, Byron and Lena do not
provide enough counterbalance to the figures of darkness.
But by virtue of the simplicity of their natures, the slow
rhythm of their lives, and the humor of their situations and
personalities, they offer some relief from the tension and
malaise that grip the novel in a vise.

Byron Bunch is a delightful character. One of Faulkner's
hillfolk, he is a humble, steady worker and a decent, self-
effacing Christian. He is like Cash Bundren in his stead-
fastness and honesty, though he is more human and appealing. Portrayed with humor and affection, Byron is the novel's
lover. He has the loyal, single-minded devotion of Faulkner's
simple people. He seems very much like Hawkshaw the
barber, the modest hero of "Hair" (May 1931) and "Dry
September" (January 1931). In "Hair" Hawkshaw waited
patiently for years to marry a girl who grew up to become
the town whore; in "Dry September" Hawkshaw was the
only white to protest against the lynching of a Negro. With
the unassuming Christianity of a Hawkshaw, Byron sought
to stir the dying embers of Hightower's conscience into life.
Byron represents the simple decency of the Southern countryman that, Faulkner hopes, will yet prevail against the Doc
Hineses and the Percy Grimms.

Byron was Hightower's link to life, while Lena was Byron's.
Unlike Joanna Burden, whose "pregnancy" proved to be a
"halfdeath," Lena was woman in her most natural and traditional role: she was mother and bearer of life, *"the good
stock peopling in tranquil obedience to it the good earth"*

(356). By giving birth to her child in the Christmas cabin, she seemed to lift the curse from the Burden plantation, which had been plagued—like its owner, Miss Burden—by barrenness and decay. The child's birth, assisted by the minister, comes like a burst of light, as if the bright augmenting dawn were celebrating the return of life and hope to mankind. Even Hightower partakes of this sense of triumph, as though he too, at least for the moment, were part of life. Born on the day that Christmas dies and identified by Mrs. Hines with her Joey, the child seems the symbol of the light that has replaced the darkness.

But neither the light radiated by the coming of the child nor the light associated with the plain, natural lives of Lena and Byron disperses the darkness that resides at the heart of the novel. For a Joe Christmas the simple Christianity of a Byron and the natural serenity of a Lena are of little avail. The tensions of Christmas' life are irresoluble. He lives and dies as the mulatto rejected by a white society, as an unregenerate rebel against society and God, and as the man who never discovers his identity. The Southern extremists, Hines and Grimm, would kill him; the Yankee sympathizer, Miss Burden, would bed with him. Obsessed by an abstraction, these people cannot understand the Negro as human being; and the Negro, in turn, cannot respond as human being. Much of the fanaticism may be traced to the intense, puritanical identification with God characteristic of Doc Hines, McEachern, and Miss Burden; their Calvinism—it varies with each—is depicted as negatively obsessed with sex and devoid of humanity. Yet the immolation, inhumanity, and righteous self-justification of their religion, Faulkner seems to say, are part of Southern Protestantism. As Hightower listens in his memory to the rich strains of the Sunday evening organ music, it speaks to him, like all Protestant music, not of love and life but of immolation and death. "He seems to hear within it the apotheosis of his own history, his own land, his own environed blood" (322). The religion of his people, he believes, drives them "*to crucifixion of themselves and one another*" (322); they will crucify Christmas and even raise a cross to him, " 'since to pity him would be to admit selfdoubt and to hope for and need pity themselves. They will do it gladly, gladly. That's why it is so terrible, terrible, terrible' " (322).

Although Christmas' death seems a crucifixion, is it not also a form of suicide? His submission to pain and death reflects a lifelong pattern of masochism: the punishment he waited to receive from the dietitian; the McEachern whippings to which he submitted as if his "body might have been wood or stone; a post or a tower upon which the sentient part of him mused like a hermit, contemplative and remote with ecstasy and selfcrucifixion" (139-140); and the beatings he provoked and took and paid back to the others. His suffering is sadistic as well as masochistic, for he was both hitting back at the world and punishing himself. The man and woman this orphan killed were, in a sense, the father and mother he had never had. Rejected and rejecting, he suffers as a result of circumstance and choice. His suffering is not sacrificial, for there is no one he loves and nothing in which he believes.

In his loneliness and estrangement, Joe Christmas resembles other of Faulkner's isolated heroes: Bayard Sartoris, Quentin Compson, and, to a lesser degree, Horace Benbow. The despair that drove Bayard to violence and Quentin to masochism, the abhorrence of female sexuality that obsessed Quentin and Horace—both operated in Christmas' life too. All four men were rebelling in their own way against society and were running from others and themselves to death or defeat. All four were a combination of victim and rebel. For the most part the author laid the burden of blame upon a brutal and corrupt society. The external enemy of these men was their society, the internal enemy was their malaise. Yet their malaise in its urge to isolation and self-destruction ruled them. Hence the "Christlike" pattern of their lives was basically self-imposed. They sought death rather than life, and in their death resides no salvation.

Although Christmas' suffering stirs pity, the feelings of separation and irreconciliation he generates are so strong that the novel is denied catharsis. Joe Christmas personifies the alienation and division characteristic of our century—so much so that he seems more a state of mind than a man. Faulkner's treatment of this state of mind in *Light in August* reveals his increased awareness of man's need of human communion, for the author does not rationalize Christmas' state of mind as he did Quentin's and Horace's. Now Faulkner shows himself aware of the dehumanization that attends isolation and of the power for evil that isolation breeds. Yet Faulkner shows himself aware too of the inhumanity that lives in the heart of a society divided by race. "In *Light in August* a new voice is heard, partly Faulkner's own and partly, as it were, an over-voice speaking for the conscience of a people,"[11] sounding a note of social anguish, asking for pity and forbearance. The alienated self was Faulkner's subject in this novel, but his perspective was becoming that of the conscience of his people.

---

[11] Irving Howe, *William Faulkner: A Critical Study*, p.157.

6

Absalom, Absalom!

Seven years after the publication of *The Sound and the Fury* came *Absalom, Absalom!* (1936). *The Sound and the Fury* dealt with the fall of a family, *Absalom* deals with the fall of a society. The Quentin Compson of *Absalom* is not quite the same as the earlier Quentin: his concern is social rather than personal and his role is identified for the most part with a central quest in the novel—the quest to discover the truth about the rise and fall of his South. In its search for the truth about a whole society, the novel circles and shuttles back and forth in time, its sentences twist and strain, and its narrators attempt to re-create a past on the basis of some fact and much conjecture. Sometimes the narrators mislead unintentionally, sometimes they contradict one another, and often they are carried away by their own bias, preoccupation, or imagination. Admittedly, it is hard to come by truth, but still one might question whether a novel whose pitch is too shrill, whose approach is emotional and poetic, whose perspective seems unclear and shifting—one might question whether such a work presents the best way of getting at historical truth. The method of narration apparently mirrors not only the difficulty in getting at truth but the struggle to face truth. For all its straining, its complexities and obscurities, *Absalom*, I would conclude, is Faulkner's most historical novel.

Its intention, Ilse Dusoir Lind has said,

is to create, through the utilization of all the resources of fiction, a grand tragic vision of historic dimensions. As in the tragedies of the ancients and in the great myths of the Old Testament, the action represents issues of timeless moral significance. That Faulkner here links the decline of a social order to an infraction of fundamental morality cannot be doubted. Sutpen falls through innate deficiency of moral insight, but the error which he commits is also socially derived and thus illustrates the flaw which dooms with equal finality the aspirations of a whole culture.[1]

For Mrs. Lind and most other critics, Sutpen is the South.[2] Yet some influential critics have qualified or contradicted this interpretation. Both Malcolm Cowley and Robert Penn Warren have stated in effect that "the Deep South was settled partly by aristocrats like the Sartoris clan and partly by new men like Colonel Sutpen."[3] Whereas they see Sutpen as

---

[1] Ilse Dusoir Lind, "The Design and Meaning of *Absalom, Absalom!*," in Frederick J. Hoffman and Olga W. Vickery (eds.), *William Faulkner: Three Decades of Criticism*, p.278.

[2] For example, Mrs. Vickery treats Sutpen as "a mirror image of the South," O'Connor as "the essence of the history of the South"; Howe regards *Absalom* as the "story of the fall of the homeland," Sullivan as the "complete statement of Southern ambition, execution and success, guilt, doom and destruction in one novel," Hoffman as "the vision of the South as a whole (or of human society itself) as a creation of this selfish and impulsive drive," and Waggoner as both "a lyric evocation of the Southern past" and "a search for the truth about human life as that truth may be discovered by understanding the past." See Olga W. Vickery, *The Novels of William Faulkner*, pp.92-95; William Van O'Connor, *The Tangled Fire of William Faulkner*, pp.94-96; Irving Howe, *William Faulkner: A Critical Study*, p.161; Walter Sullivan, "The Tragic Design of *Absalom, Absalom!*," *South Atlantic Quarterly*, 50 (Oct. 1951), p.560; Frederick J. Hoffman, *William Faulkner*, pp. 74-79; and Hyatt H. Waggoner, *William Faulkner: From Jefferson to the World*, pp.149-153.

[3] This is Cowley's statement, which Warren paraphrases. See Malcolm Cowley, "Introduction to *The Portable Faulkner*," and Robert Penn Warren, "William Faulkner" in *William Faulkner: Three Decades of Criticism*, pp.102 and 111 respectively.

only partly representative of the Deep South, Cleanth Brooks would question whether Sutpen is a Southerner at all. For Brooks, Sutpen is in many ways a Yankee: he "is a 'planner' who works by blueprint and on a schedule. He is rationalistic and scientific, not traditional, not religious, not even superstitious." "Indeed, Sutpen is at some points more nearly allied to Flem [Snopes] than he is to the Compsons and the Sartorises. Like Flem, he is a new man with no concern for the past and has a boundless energy with which to carry out his aggressive plans."[4] In seeing Sutpen as basically different from the other Yoknapatawpha planters and in associating him with the Snopeses, Brooks is making use of certain stereotypes that have been best described by George Marion O'Donnell:

In Mr. Faulkner's mythology there are two kinds of characters; they are Sartorises or Snopeses, whatever the family names may be. And in the spiritual geography of Mr. Faulkner's work there are two worlds: the Sartoris world and the Snopes world. In all of his successful books, he is exploring the two worlds in detail, dramatizing the inevitable conflict between them.

It is a universal conflict. The Sartorises act traditionally; that is to say, they act always with an ethically responsible will. They represent vital morality, humanism. Being anti-traditional, the Snopeses are immoral from the Sartoris point of view. But the Snopeses do not recognize this point of view; acting only for self-interest, they acknowledge no ethical duty. Really, then, they are amoral; they represent naturalism or animalism. And the Sartoris-Snopes conflict is fundamentally a struggle between humanism and naturalism.[5]

Such a view—with its simplistic division of the South into Sartorises and Snopeses, its blindness to the guilt and tension

---

[4] Cleanth Brooks, *William Faulkner: The Yoknapatawpha Country*, pp.306, 307.

[5] George Marion O'Donnell, "Faulkner's Mythology," in *Three Decades of Criticism*, pp.83-84.

and ambivalence which beset its Quentin Compsons—maps the reality neither of the historical South nor of Yoknapatawpha. It would, in fact, shut out reality and substitute legend; it would reduce the complexity of human life and character to a single abstraction. Contrary to the Sartoris-Snopes thesis, the antebellum South, though once ruled by the planter class, did not consist only of planter aristocracy and poor whites; the great majority of its people have always been hard-working small farmers,[6] like the Tulls and Bundrens and Houstons and Quicks and Armstids of Yoknapatawpha. Moreover, to attribute the decline of the South to the Snopeses is to compound legend with fantasy, for not only does such a view assume the existence of an aristocratic South based on a benevolent system of slavery and characterized by humanistic values but it finds a ready scapegoat for its ills in a tribe of Southern "Yankees," the Snopeses. It is more logical and just to assign the major responsibility for the fortunes of the South to its rulers—the Thomas Sutpens. And it is essential, if we are to understand *Absalom*, to know (1) the fact and legend of Southern history and (2) how Sutpen's life and career mirror the history and heritage of the South, moral as well as social and political.

Northern Mississippi was settled in the 1830's and 1840's. Mississippi did not become a state until 1817, and the town of Oxford, generally accepted as the prototype for Jefferson, was still an Indian trading post in 1835.[7] De Tocqueville, who

---

[6] Avery Craven, *The Growth of Southern Nationalism, 1848-1861* (Baton Rouge, Louisiana State University, 1953), p.11; Avery Craven, *The Coming of the Civil War* (New York, Scribners, 1950), pp.26-29; and Herbert Weaver, *Mississippi Farmers, 1850-1860* (Nashville, Tenn., Vanderbilt University, 1945), pp.11-13, 28-29, 41, 48 and 57.

[7] Charles Sackett Sydnor, *Slavery in Mississippi* (New York, Appleton-Century, 1933), pp.41, 247-248; and Ward L. Miner, *The World of William Faulkner* (Durham, N.C., Duke University, 1952), pp. 18-36.

travelled through America in the 1830's, described Southwestern society as "only an agglomeration of adventurers
and speculators,"[8] and Baldwin's *The Flush Times of Alabama and Mississippi* (1853) confirms de Tocqueville's appraisal. Historians generally agree that the Deep South, right
up to the Civil War, was largely frontier country.[9] W. J. Cash,
for example, describes the making of the great or Deep
South in this manner:

1810 came and went, the battle of New Orleans was fought and
won, and it was actually 1820 before the plantation was fully on
the march, striding over the hills of Carolina to Mississippi—
1820 before the tide of immigration was in full sweep about the
base of the Appalachians.

From 1820 to 1860 is but forty years—a little more than the
span of a single generation. The whole period from the invention
of the cotton gin to the outbreak of the Civil War is less than
seventy years—the lifetime of a single man. Yet it was wholly
within the longer of these periods, and mainly within the shorter,
that the development and growth of the great South took place.
Men who, as children, had heard the war-whoop of the Cherokee
in the Carolina backwoods lived to hear the guns at Vicksburg.
And thousands of other men who had looked upon Alabama when
it was still a wilderness and upon Mississippi when it was still a
stubborn jungle, lived to fight—and to fight well, too—in the ranks
of the Confederate armies.

The inference is plain. It is impossible to conceive the great
South as being, on the whole, more than a few steps removed
from the frontier stage at the beginning of the Civil War. It is
imperative, indeed, to conceive it as having remained more or less

[8] Alexis de Tocqueville, *Democracy in America,* ed. Phillips Bradley
(New York, Knopf, 1946), I, 204.

[9] See, for example, Howard W. Odum, *The Way of the South* (New
York, Macmillan, 1947), p.23; Vernon Lane Wharton, *The Negro in
Mississippi, 1865-1890* (Chapel Hill, University of North Carolina,
1947), p.216; and Avery Craven, *The Coming of the Civil War,* pp.
25-27.

fully in the frontier stage for a great part—maybe the greater
part—of its antebellum history.[10]

If this is so, who were the aristocrats of the Deep South?
For the great part, they were "but the natural flower of the
backcountry grown prosperous."[11] In Mississippi before 1860
a white man could lay claim to the title of gentry if he acquired the land and the slaves. The importance of the established gentry of the Carolina, Tidewater, and Natchez plantations lay not in their migration to the undeveloped South
but in the potency of their influence upon the South's lower
classes. Although some planters or their sons did come to
the lower South, most of the men pushing into the Mississippi
wilderness were from the backwoods. The plantation aristocracy served them as a symbol and goal, as the crown of a
Southerner's achievement; it provided the more successful
and ambitious with a manner and tradition which they put
on, so to speak, like a new cloak. But after the Civil War the
South, "beset by the specters of defeat, of shame, of guilt,"
submerged the fact and romanticized the claim of the
planter.[12] Hence was spread the legend of the Old South:

the legend of which the backbone is, of course, precisely the
assumption that every planter was in the most rigid sense of the
word a gentleman.

Enabling the South to wrap itself in a contemptuous superiority, to sneer down the Yankee as low-bred, crass, and money-

---

[10] W. J. Cash, *The Mind of the South* (Garden City, Doubleday,
1954), p.24.

[11] Ibid., p.33. See also Frank Lawrence Owsley, *Plain Folk of the
Old South* (Baton Rouge, Louisiana State University, 1949), p.90.

[12] Cash, p.73. See also Craven, *The Coming of the Civil War*, pp.
17-18; and Sydnor, *Slavery in Mississippi*, p.248.

grubbing, and even to beget in his bougeois soul a kind of secret and envious awe, it was a nearly perfect defense-mechanism.[13]

Under the spur of the Civil War defeat, the Southerner's need to believe in the aristocracy of his ancestors and in the superiority of his tradition hastened the spread of the Southern legend. The legend affected the whole South, not just the Deep South. The force of its need and conviction submerged the fact that almost no members of the Cavalier aristocracy ever left England for America, that the Southern aristocracy derived from the low and middle classes, and that the aristocracy of the Deep South was made in one generation.[14] Scratch the veneer of the aristocrat of the Deep South and you would find a frontiersman. It was these new planters who took over the leadership of the Old South. The Natchez and Virginia gentry, longer exposed and hence more susceptible to the opinion of the rest of the Western world, were less able to conceive of slavery as a "positive good." But the new men brought to their position the frontier's aggressiveness,

---

[13] Cash, p.73.

[14] Historians have long recognized that the Cavalier and planter legends derive from wishful thinking rather than fact. For early research on the subject, see Thomas Jefferson Wertenbaker, *Patrician and Plebeian in Virginia* (Charlottesville, privately printed, 1910), Preface and pp.1-21 [Recent editions of his works have been published by Russell & Russell]; and G. W. Dyer, *Democracy in the South Before the Civil War* (Nashville, Methodist Episcopal Church, South, 1905), pp.30-34. Although Wertenbaker established convincingly the non-aristocratic origins of the Virginia gentry, W. J. Cash, writing a generation later, had to explode the myth again. For other historical commentary, see Avery Craven, *The Coming of the Civil War*, pp.17-34; C. Vann Woodward, *The Burden of Southern History* (Baton Rouge, Louisiana State University, 1960), pp.12-13; and William R. Taylor, *Cavalier and Yankee* (New York, Braziller, 1961), pp.17-18, 67, 96, 146-148, 203-205 and 334-341.

The general acceptance of the Sartoris-Snopes interpretation of Faulkner's works suggests that the myth, in another form, still lives with us.

the strength and ruthlessness of self-made men, and a fierce
faith in the righteousness of their cause and their interests.
Nine-tenths of the men who directed the affairs of the Confederate government, like nine-tenths of the men who of-
ficered its armies, says Cash, were not Colonial aristocrats
but new people.[15]

With the possible exception of Sartoris, all the founders
of the ruling clans in Yoknapatawpha were new men. Sutpen,
McCaslin, and Compson got their land by hook or by crook.
Compson acquired his by swapping a mare to the Indians,
Sutpen got his with a little Spanish gold, and McCaslin
"bought the land, took the land, got the land no matter
how."[16] Faulkner has not told us how Sarioris got his land,
but Sartoris possessed the "violent and ruthless dictatorial-
ness and will to dominate"[17] which generally characterize the
founders of the Yoknapatawpha ruling clans. The getting of
the land, the hacking of a plantation out of the wilderness,
and the establishment of a family dynasty would naturally
promote violence, ruthlessness, and strength of character,
and not "vital morality and humanism."

Nevertheless, Faulkner does make a distinction between
Sartoris and Sutpen. They are different, not in the sense that
Sartoris was an established Yoknapatawpha planter when
Sutpen arrived at Jefferson in 1833—Sartoris did not arrive

---

[15] Cash, p.71. Avery Craven states: "A careful study of biographical
materials and facts revealed in the manuscript census shows that only
some 7.73 per cent of the men who represented Virginia, the Carolinas,
Alabama, Mississippi, Louisiana, Georgia, and Tennessee in the House
and Senate from 1850 to 1860 were plantation owners or had come
from families of plantation owners." Craven, *The Growth of Southern
Nationalism*, p.163.

[16] William Faulkner, *Go Down, Moses, and Other Stories* (New
York, Random House, 1942), p.256.

[17] William Faulkner, *The Unvanquished* (New York, Random
House, 1938), p.258. These words are voiced silently by Colonel
Sartoris' son as he broods over his father's character.

until a few years after Sutpen[18]—but in the sense that Sartoris'
origin was "aristocratic" whereas Sutpen's was plebeian.
Colonel Sartoris, as we see him in *Sartoris* and later in *The
Unvanquished,* is a much more traditionally romantic figure
than Sutpen. Sartoris, it is generally acknowledged, is mod-
eled in part on the character and life of the author's great-
grandfather, Colonel William C. Falkner. Yet Falkner's origin
more closely approximates that of Sutpen than of Sartoris:
Sartoris came to Mississippi "with slaves and gear and
money"[19] from a Carolina plantation, but Falkner came
out of Tennessee as a poor boy. The inference is plain:
Sartoris represents in part a projection of the legend, but
Sutpen represents the reality.

To get at the reality, however, would be difficult for Faulkner, difficult because he would not only have to work his
way out of the distortions wrought by Southern legend and
pride but he would have to repudiate the uncritical allegiance
and assent demanded by a closed society even though it was
still his home and native land. Yet the story, he said, "wouldn't
let me alone"; he had to write it.[20] Next to *The Sound and
the Fury, Absalom* was, admittedly, the novel that gave him
the most trouble, the novel that apparently sprang out of
compulsion and reluctance, out of pride and guilt, out of love
and hate. The character in *Absalom* that expresses these ambivalent feelings is of course Quentin Compson. Without
Quentin the story would never be told. He brings together
all the facts and conjectures about Sutpen, he is the story's
compelled listener and narrator, and he cares most about

---

[18] William Faulkner, *Requiem for a Nun* (New York, Random
House, 1951), p.44.

[19] Ibid.

[20] *Faulkner in the University,* ed. by Frederick L. Gwynn and Joseph
L. Blotner, p.281.

what Sutpen signifies.[21] "Out of the rag-tag and bob-ends of old tales and talking,"[22] out of Miss Rosa's "demonizing" and his father's speculating, he must reconstruct a past that might have been, a man that apparently was. He must because the man in a sense was his ancestor, the past his past and present too.

The man, like almost all the aristocrats of the Deep South, began his life at the frontier. Most settlers of the South were descended from the English and "the half-wild Scotch and Irish clansmen of the seventeenth and eighteenth centuries,"[23] and some of course came from the house of Old Bailey.[24] Thomas Sutpen was born in the mountains of west Virginia, his mother a Scottish mountain woman, his father an ex-prisoner of the Old Bailey. In the mountains "the land belonged to anybody and everybody and so the man who would go to the trouble and work to fence off a piece of it and say 'This is mine' was crazy" (221). At the frontier it was

---

[21] Many critics have recognized that the Sutpen story is Quentin's story too, that its full meaning does not make itself felt until the story has impacted upon Quentin's brooding, Hamlet-like conscience. The very tension between Quentin and what he is hearing and telling gives the novel its peculiar shading and significance. Faulkner himself has said that *Absalom* is both the story of Sutpen and "the story of Quentin Compson's hatred of the bad qualities in the country he loves" (*Faulkner in the University*, p.71). A good analysis of this aspect of *Absalom* may be found in an essay by Richard B. Sewall, *The Vision of Tragedy* (New Haven, Conn., Yale, 1959), pp.133-147.

[22] *Absalom, Absalom!* (New York, Modern Library, 1951), p.303. All quotations from *Absalom* are from this edition.

[23] Cash, p.42. See also Owsley, *Plain Folk of the Old South*, pp.90-91.

[24] That Faulkner places little stock in the genealogical claims of Southerners may be inferred not only from the origins he assigns to Sutpen but from the words he puts into the mouth of Sartoris himself: " 'In the nineteenth century . . . genealogy is poppycock. Particularly in America, where only what a man takes and keeps has any significance and where all of us have a common ancestry and the only house from which we can claim descent with any assurance is the Old Bailey.' " *Sartoris* (New York, Harcourt, Brace, 1929), p.92.

not possessions but physical strength that determined one's worth, the strength "to be measured by lifting anvils or gouging eyes or how much whiskey you could drink then get up and walk out of the room" (226). But at the mother's death the Sutpen family lost its hold upon their mountain home, "slid back down out of the mountains" (223), and "fell" (222) into a "land divided neatly up and actually owned by men who did nothing but ride over it on fine horses or sit in fine clothes on the galleries of big houses while other people worked for them" (221). That the journey from the highland to the lowland, from the democratic way of life of the frontier to the stratified plantation society of the Tidewater region was a fall is confirmed by the disintegration of the Sutpen family and the decline of their pride. The boy Thomas Sutpen saw his mother dead, his father transported in a drunken stupor, his brothers vanishing, his sister giving birth to two nameless bastards, and their home become a rotting cabin. In a futile attempt to salvage something of their frontier pride the father whipped one of Pettibone's "niggers," and the sister sullenly refused to give way to a planter's carriage. But the unhappy transition from frontier independence to sharecropping subservience could not be effaced by violence against the Negro or by an occasional gesture against the planter. Now a man's worth was measured not by his manhood but by his possessions.

It was this humiliating truth that broke abruptly in upon the young Sutpen's innocence after the white door of the planter's mansion closed upon him and the "monkey nigger" told him to go around to the back. Retreating to a kind of cave in the woods, he brooded upon the meaning of this rejection. For the first time in his life he saw "his own father and sisters and brothers as the owner, the rich man (not the nigger) must have been seeing them all the time—as cattle, creatures heavy and without grace, brutely evacuated into a world without hope or purpose for them" (235). All that day he looked through his hurt into the face of the world's reality, until he knew that the only way to combat the world was to get for himself the land, the slaves, and the fine house upon which the planter had established his power and glory. He went to the island of Haiti to get what he wanted. He did not know that this "little lost island" (253) had been "manured with black blood" and "torn limbs and outraged hearts" (251). Like the single-minded Ahab, he knew only what he wanted. Crushing a slave rebellion, he rose from overseer to planter's son-in-law, and then to owner of land and house and slaves.

The decision that Sutpen made as a boy becomes the fateful decision of his life: he gave up the values of the frontier for those of a property-caste system. It was a decision full of bitter ironies, for in time it would lead to a war in which the backwoodsman fought by the side of the planter to preserve a system alien to his character and heritage. The planter and backwoodsman were separated by long-standing differences, but in the fierce mounting tension between North and South and in the War and its bitter aftermath, Southerners suppressed their differences. Still the union between planter and backwoodsman, despite its surface solidarity, remained fundamentally uneasy. Faulkner's own sympathies seemed to be on the side of the backwoodsman. Although Faulkner depicted the frontier way of life as crude and often brutal, he presented it as basically more honest and natural and innocent, simply because it was not founded on and sustained by property, by slavery. Ultimately, Sutpen's decision is a moral one: he committed the sin that would visit the iniquity of the father upon the children, and upon the children's children, unto the third and to the fourth generation. He did not know what he was doing, he would never know.

In 1829 Sutpen got his son. He named him Charles Bon—

a name ironically reminiscent of Bonnie Prince Charlie, who
was heir to a throne he never inherited and prince to a
nation that repudiated him. In 1831 Sutpen repudiated his
"Negro" wife and son. The repudiation of the Negro was
compelled by the planter's "design." Yet the repudiation
planted the seed of the system's destruction. Charles Bon
represents both the doomed victim and fated undoer of the
"design." He incarnates in a sense the tragic history of the
American Negro. Running through his veins was the blood
of the slavers and planters—the Spanish, French, English, and
American—and the blood of the African Negro. But it was
the Negro blood that would work like a strange power of
fate in the lives of the planters, the slaves, and all their
descendants.

Two decades after Columbus' discovery of the New
World, Negro slaves were working in the sugar plantations
of Haiti. Shortly thereafter Negro slavery spread to the mainland of America. The Renaissance and the Commercial Revolution had unleashed new energies and freedoms; one of them
was "the freedom to destroy freedom." The enslaving and
trading and working of Negroes were a principal means by
which the newly powerful nation-states of Europe exploited
the New World and filled their coffers. As Portugal, Spain,
Holland, France, and England struggled in the next few
centuries to expand their interests in the new hemisphere,
the Negro slave became the pawn in the struggle. By the
first quarter of the eighteenth century England was taking
over most of the world's slave trade, and slavery was becoming a cornerstone in her economic prosperity. The West
Indies, whose sugar plantations in the seventeenth century
had been Britain's chief source of wealth in the New World,
were now yielding their economic primacy to the mainland.
In the American colonies, particularly in Virginia and the

Carolinas, slavery continued to grow throughout the century. In the decade before the American Revolution, the colonists blamed the British crown for slavery. But, ironically enough, it was the United States, founded on and dedicated to equality and freedom, that became the arena for the greatest expansion of slavery the world had ever seen. Stimulated by a seemingly inexhaustible demand for cotton, which the Industrial Revolution had created, and enabled by Whitney's new invention to separate quickly the seed from the fiber, Southerners moved westward in search for new land to plant cotton. The southwestern lands were rich and ready to be taken. All that was needed was labor. Virginia, its soil exhausted by tobacco, had plenty of slaves and could in time breed more, and there were always the West Indies and Africa from which slaves could be smuggled into the United States. So was born the Cotton Kingdom.[25]

Thomas Sutpen, who transplanted his slaves from Haiti to the Mississippi wilderness and transformed the wilderness to a plantation, was part of a large historical movement. He was part of the movement of slavery from the islands to the mainland and from the Eastern seaboard to the Southwest. Paradoxically, slavery was to find its most aggressive defenders in the Southern democrats of the United States. The very aggressiveness of the defense was related to various factors. For the Western world the nineteenth century was a century of industrial progress and intellectual liberalism, but for the South it was a century of resistance to the tide of liberalism and progress. Isolated, feeling itself threatened by a growing and hostile North, and harboring a bad conscience over its peculiar system, the South grew more ready

---

[25] John Hope Franklin, *From Slavery to Freedom* (New York, Knopf, 1952), pp.42-183; and W. E. Burghardt Du Bois, *Black Folk: Then and Now* (New York, Holt, 1939), pp.126-144.

to turn to violence. C. Vann Woodward, the Southern historian, has commented upon the South's state of mind immediately prior to the Civil War:

The South had been living in a crisis atmosphere for a long time. It was a society in the grip of an insecurity complex, a tension resulting from both rational and irrational fears. One cause of it was the steady, invincible expansion of the free-state system in size and power, after the Southern system had reached the limits of its own expansion. The South, therefore, felt itself to be menaced through encirclement by a power containing elements unfriendly to its interests, elements that were growing strong enough to capture the government. The South's insecurity was heightened by having to defend against constant attack an institution it knew to be discredited throughout the civilized world and of which Southerners had once been among the severest critics. Its reaction was to withdraw increasingly from contact with the offending world, to retreat into an isolationism of spirit, and to attempt by curtailing freedom of speech to avoid criticism.[26]

"Much of the South's intellectual energy," Woodward continues, "went into a desperate effort to convince the world that its peculiar evil was actually a 'positive good,' but it failed even to convince itself. It writhed in the torments of its own conscience until it plunged into catastrophe to escape."[27] According to Woodward, the South, beset by a bad conscience, turned guilt and frustration into aggression and destruction. Woodward may be exaggerating the role played by conscience. We must remember that in the generation preceding the outbreak of the Civil War, the South was expanding: the frontier was being pushed westward and southward, the Cotton Kingdom was growing into the chief economic and social fact of the South's existence, and political power was shifting from Virginia and the Carolinas

[26] C. Vann Woodward, *The Burden of Southern History*, p.62.
[27] Ibid., pp.20-21.

to the Deep South. The men who were making this expansion were caught up in the grip of their own ambitions and interests. They were passionate rather than reflective, doers rather than thinkers. Simply and fiercely they identified themselves and their interests with the South. Their proneness to violence was probably due less to bad conscience than to the fact that violence had played an important role in their frontier background and in their making of a plantation. It was a time when the South chose not a Thomas Jefferson but a Jefferson Davis as its leader. It was a time of Thomas Sutpens, not Quentin Compsons.

In the 1830's the men who would later become the leaders of the South in the Civil War were men on the make, men who had yet to achieve their dream. It was a "dream of grim and castlelike magnificence" (38) which Thomas Sutpen, with the help of his slaves and the captured French architect, built into the great house itself. With an assist from the puritan, Goodhue Coldfield, he acquired the appropriate furnishings for his baronial dream: the chandeliers, rugs, mahogany, and "the stainless wife" (51). The marriage of Thomas Sutpen to Ellen Coldfield signifies the union of frontiersman and puritan, a union which would give birth to the very character of the South. Frontier violence would be yoked to fundamentalist religion, frontier individualism would be wedded to the puritan's conscience. Superimposed on the marriage was the plantation system, with another set of values and with its Peculiar Institution.

In Mississippi the planter-to-be had no time to waste. Out of the virgin land Sutpen "tore violently a plantation" (9), and out of the virgin wife "without gentleness begot" (9) a son and daughter. He was hurrying his dream into shape. Even the names of his offspring and possessions reflect the dream. Charles and Henry might have come from English and Norman royalty, Judith from the Old Testament, Clytemnestra from the Greeks, and Rob Roy (his thoroughbred stallion) from Sir Walter Scott. By the 1850's Sutpen had become the biggest landowner and planter of Yoknapatawpha. "He acted his role too—a role of arrogant ease and leisure" (72), while his wife "moved, lived, from attitude to attitude against her background of chatelaine to the largest, wife to the wealthiest, mother of the most fortunate" (69). Dream had become actuality. "Now he would take that boy in where he would never again need to stand on the outside of a white door" (261). He had riven himself free from the brutehood of his past, made himself part of the proud and privileged class of the South, and had planted the heir who would perpetuate the achievement. So it seemed—until the Christmas of 1859 when retribution knocked on the white door of Sutpen's great house, and the past he had put away walked back into his life in the person of his first son, Charles Bon.

Charles Bon. Charles Good. In station and manners and breeding he was the elegant New Orleans scion, fortunate member of the planter class and an elite Latin culture. In personality he was "gentle sardonic whimsical and incurably pessimistic" (129). In his heart he was the son whose life had been "enclosed by an unsleeping cabal bent apparently on teaching him that he had never had a father" (313), he was "that mental and spiritual orphan whose fate it apparently was to exist in some limbo" (124), he was that "forlorn nameless and homeless lost child" (267) who came knocking on the white door of Sutpen's house. He wanted no inheritance; he wanted but a word, a sign, a look, a touch from Sutpen which would say you are my son. He got no acknowledgment, he got nothing. Even the love he got from his brother Henry turned into ashes when Henry learned that Bon was "the nigger that's going to sleep with your sister" (358). For all his sophistication, Bon remained only the orphan (he never really had a mother since, warped by paranoiac hatred of Sutpen, she had lost the power to love) who never found the father he sought: that was his fate. So it was that he lived as if something had gone out of him, as if he did not really want to live.

The story of Charles Bon is a richly ironic fable of the Old South. Bon embodies both the most favored of whites, a New Orleans scion, and the lowliest of blacks, the white man's bastard. He is the intelligent, cultivated young gentleman who must be shot by a Mississippi clodhopper because the nigger signifies a subhuman threat to white womanhood. Like his father, he cannot acknowledge his son by a colored woman. These ironies are part of a system; beneath these ironies rest other parts of the system's foundation. In the Old South the Negro slave had generally no father and little mother. Under a system that made human beings into chattels, the Negro woman, when she did not labor in the fields, served as the breeder of stock and as the instrument for the white man's sexual pleasure. The Negress was a kind of mare, the Negro a stud. The effect was to destroy or warp the institution of the family among a whole people. In removing sex from its familial role, the system did violence to the morality of both whites and blacks.[28] It made sex for the

---

[28] It is of course difficult to appraise the moral and psychological damage done to the Negro in the process of enslaving him. One can suggest, however, some historians and commentators who provide information and insight: Frederick Bancroft, *Slave Trading in the Old South* (New York, Ungar, 1959); E. Franklin Frazier, *The Negro Family in the United States* (New York, Dryden, 1948); John Hope Franklin, *From Slavery to Freedom;* W. E. Burghardt Du Bois, *Black Folk: Then and Now;* Frank Tannenbaum, *Slave and Citizen: The Negro in the Americas* (New York, Knopf, 1947); Daniel P. Mannix, in collaboration with Malcolm Cowley, *Black Cargoes: A History of the Atlantic Slave Trade* (New York, Viking, 1962); Frederick Douglass, *Narrative of the Life of Frederick Douglass, an American Slave, Written by Himself,* edited by Benjamin Quarles (Cambridge, Belknap, 1960); and Stanley M. Elkins, *Slavery* (Chicago, University of Chicago, 1959).

Negro into an irresponsible animal relationship; it made sex for the white man into a guilty, dishonest one. A schism, a kind of unconscious hypocrisy, embedded itself deeply into the soul of the South. For the white man the Negress was the female animalized and the white woman was the female spiritualized. It was as if the planter were trying to make up to his white woman for his faithlessness and duplicity.[29] Reality was two families by the planter, white and black. Reality was a brother who was not a brother, a sister who was not a sister, a wife who was not a wife. Southerners knew of this reality, accepted it, lived with it, even though it violated what they thought they believed in: honor, pride, the family, and the decencies of life. This reality underlies the story of the House of Sutpen.

All the relationships in the Sutpen family are invested with a peculiar irony, doom, and tragedy, as if a curse had been placed on them like the curse of the House of Oedipus. Incest, fratricide, and the fall of a family are all aspects of both curses. Moreover, like several characters in *Oedipus Rex*, the Sutpens, for the most part, did not know the full truth about themselves and could not realize their identity and humanity. Henry and Charles were brothers, yet not brothers; Judith and Charles were sister and brother, yet not sister and brother; Sutpen and Charles were father and son, yet not father and son. They seem compelled as by a Greek fate—such is the power of the system—to repudiate or destroy one another; they seem compelled as by the Old Testament God to suffer for the sins of their father. It was the father, the nucleus of the culture, who determined the fate and character of the others. He signifies an elemental force, a heroic *hybris*, in the Southern culture; he is the

---

[29] See Cash, pp.97-98.

archetype of the Southern planter. There is a grandeur to the man who hammers out his "design" in the face of God's and nature's opposition. Yet there is a fatal defect too: his Adamic innocence, like that of other American barons on the make, had hardened into moral blindness, and the egoism and energy generated by his rejection and dream of vindication had become ultimately a force for destruction of himself, his family, and his society. In attempting to build a dynasty, he had lost a family; in making himself into the image of the Southern planter, he had lost part of his humanity; in displacing conscience by pride, he had lost the power to see into himself. Since he was "incapable of that rending of the self and tearing out of pride which forms the tragic element,"[30] his life ended not in tragic affirmation but in gross deterioration and unheroic death.

Ironically, the lowliest of the whites is the instrument of retribution. For Wash Jones the Colonel signified all that was best in the planter: courage, honor, paternalism, and authority. For Wash the Colonel was a god.

. . . on the week days he would see Sutpen (the fine figure of the man as he called it) on the black stallion, galloping about the plantation, and Father said how for that moment Wash's heart would be quiet and proud both and that maybe it would seem to him that this world where niggers, that the Bible said had been created and cursed by God to be brute and vassal to all men of white skin, were better found and housed and even clothed than he and his granddaughter—that this world where he walked always in mocking and jeering echoes of nigger laughter, was just a dream and an illusion and that the actual world was the one where his own lonely apotheosis (Father said) galloped on the black thoroughbred, thinking maybe, Father said, how the Book said that all men were created in the image of God and so all men were the same in God's eyes anyway, looked the same

---

[30] Howe, p.164.

to God at least, and so he would look at Sutpen and think *A fine proud man. If God Himself was to come down and ride the natural earth, that's what He would aim to look like.* (282)

In spite of the blind contradiction in Wash's belief that the Bible could be used as authority for both the Negro's enslavement and man's equality, there is something touching about Wash's faith in the planter who had sprung from the same brute origins but who in the span of several decades had become the poor white's apotheosis. By 1869, however, the ravages of the War and Reconstruction had eaten so deeply into the planter and his "design" that his power was being broken and his ruthlessness exposed. The breaking point came when Sutpen, having attended the mare that had just foaled a colt to his stallion, entered Wash's cabin to see whether he had bred a son by Milly, Wash's granddaughter. Bending over the pallet where she lay with her newborn daughter, he said, " 'Well, Milly; too bad you're not a mare too. Then I could give you a decent stall in the stable' " (286). The earth seemed to fall away from beneath Wash's feet. He confronted the planter. Like the Grim Reaper, he raised the rusty scythe; the planter's whip lashed twice across his face, and then the scythe came down.

Although the poor white has been depicted as the instrument of the planter's demise, the deterioration of Sutpen's will and character, wrought by the inroads of the War and Reconstruction, contributed also to his downfall. The planter's confidence and power had been deeply shaken by the loss of the War; nevertheless, the Southern people did not actually repudiate their leaders until much later. Toward the end of the nineteenth century they did begin to turn to other leaders, to those who made the Negro the scapegoat for the Lost Cause and the current ills. The Negro, who had once been inviolate as the planter's chattel, became fair game for any white. Providing an outlet for the people's frustration and resentment, racism became the official policy of the South. In effect, Faulkner was right: the poor white eventually did turn on the planter.

What survived from Sutpen's "design"? There was the heir apparent, Henry Sutpen, who vanished for a generation, only to reappear at the beginning of the next century like a futile ghost out of a dead but lingering past. And there were the three women: Judith, Clytie, and Rosa Coldfield. Judith had been intended "by the tradition in which Thomas Sutpen's ruthless will had carved a niche to pass through the soft insulated and unscathed cocoon stages: bud, served prolific queen, then potent and soft-handled matriarch of old age's serene and well-lived content" (156). Instead, she had become "the bowed and unwived widow kneeling" (138) beside her lover's corpse. She lived on in the empty and rotting house, scraping out a meager existence by doing a man's labor. In silent, stoic joylessness she survived the privations of the War and Reconstruction. Her mulatto sister, Clytie, continued long beyond Judith's death as the guardian of her master's house. Clytie represents the Negro family servant so involved with her white folks that she could make no life of her own. Finally there was Miss Rosa. Conceived in her parents' old age, as Gail Hightower had been, she passed from a warped childhood to a spinster's dream world and became a writer of odes to Confederate heroes. But the emotional thrust of her life derived from her hatred of Sutpen, a hatred which stemmed mainly from his matter-of-fact proposal "that they try it first and if it was a boy and lived, they would be married" (284). Faulkner's characterization of Miss Rosa is generally rendered in broad paradox and sly irony. She is both the chaste Southern woman and warped old maid; the romantic defender of the South and paranoiac hater of its supreme representative, Thomas Sutpen; vicarious bride in her dreams to Charles Bon and hater of the

Negro. So shielded had she been from the realities of the Old South, Rosa Coldfield never knew she had loved the "nigger" son of Thomas Sutpen.

The true heir of the grand "design" was Charles Etienne Saint-Valery Bon, only child of Thomas Sutpen's elder son. Neither black nor white, living in a much less fortunate time and having less than his father, he became the classic mulatto pariah. He struggled to find his identity by marrying a coal-black woman and living a Negro's life; but he could only express himself by destroying himself, by "treading the thorny and flintpaved path toward Gethsemane [sic] which he had decreed and created for himself, where he had cruci-fied himself and come down from his cross for a moment and now returned to it" (209). "With a furious and indomitable desperation" (202) he flung the gage of his apparently futile challenge in the white world's face and turned from his "emancipation" to death.

As the nineteenth century yielded to the twentieth, there survived the rotting house, its slave guardian, the death-in-life heir (Henry), and the last Sutpen descendant—the idiot, Jim Bond. It had taken two generations for Bon to become Bond, good to become slave.[31] Not much was left of the planter's baronial dream. Like the planter's mansion, the dream kept rotting. In December 1909 the house of Sutpen went up in smoke. Only the idiot remained. The others were dead. Dead was the planter with his double family, black and white; dead were the Coldfields, with the shopkeeper's barren puritanism and the spinster's barren gentility; and dead was the poor white family of Wash Jones.

A mood of despair and futility pervades this story of the South. Even the most decent of men, General Compson, could only conclude when touched by the misery and de-

---

31 I am indebted to Konrad Hopkins for this idea.

structiveness of Valery Bon's life, " *'Better that he were dead, better that he had never lived'* " (205). Yet the despair has been quickened by a kind of fierce, underground idealism. Valery Bon destroyed himself not only because he would rather be dead but because he felt compelled to make a protest against the system which denies his people their human rights. Even Wash Jones's life ended in protest. From an outraged and anguished heart Faulkner has cried out in *Absalom* against an evil implanted in his South.

Faulkner has presented Sutpen as the source of the evil, but he has presented him too as the only heroic figure in the story. Sutpen is both the pride and the shame of the South. For a Quentin Compson the ambivalence of his feelings about his heritage is further complicated by the reality of the present. His heritage is peculiarly compounded of accomplishment and defeat, innocence and guilt, pride and defensiveness. The ruthless planter-backwoodsman who built his house upon slavery and lived as if the evil were a positive good is dead and gone. For his descendants accomplishment has often become but a memory, pride has become delusion, and innocence has become unacknowledgeable guilt. As loyalty to the Old South has turned into savage racism, the planter's power to act has deteriorated for his twentieth-century descendants into a stasis of will.

For Quentin, as for his father, Sutpen represented another time when men were

simpler and therefore, integer for integer, larger, more heroic and the figures therefore more heroic too, not dwarfed and involved but distinct, uncomplex who had the gift of loving once or dying once instead of being diffused and scattered creatures drawn blindly limb from limb from a grab bag and assembled. . . (89)

Out of his sense of impotence and alienation, Quentin, like Bon himself, seemed to turn to the godlike Sutpen for the power and virility he lacked, for the father who would solve the son's dilemma. But the giant, rising out of the past like a swiftly growing djinn from Aladdin's lamp, threatened to consume rather than renew the puny summoner. The vision of the South which Quentin invoked left him shivering, "panting in the cold air, the iron New England dark; *I dont. I dont! I dont hate it! I dont hate it!*" (378). Even in the alien air of New England the South was too much with him. The burden of its history lay heavy upon Quentin Compson. Torn by loyalty and guilt, by the desire to defend and the need to expiate, by the desire to suppress and the need to confess, he could only cry out against his burden. And this is how the novel ends—with the sins of the past unexpiated and the dilemma of the present irresoluble.

7

The Unvanquished

Faulkner's concern with the South and its past continued in *The Unvanquished* (1938). *The Unvanquished* is a collection of seven related stories that tell about the Sartoris family during the Civil War and Reconstruction era. These stories—with the exception of the last, "An Odor of Verbena"—were originally published between 1934 and 1936 in the *Saturday Evening Post* and *Scribner's Magazine*.[1] Although *The Unvanquished* shows some revisions of the magazine stories, in their final form the stories remain basically unchanged in plot, theme, and character.[2] If one com-

---

[1] The stories first appeared as follows: "Ambuscade," *Saturday Evening Post*, Sept. 29, 1934; "Retreat," *Saturday Evening Post*, Oct. 13, 1934; "Raid," *Saturday Evening Post*, Nov. 3, 1934; "Riposte in Tertio" (published originally under the title "The Unvanquished"), *Saturday Evening Post*, Nov. 14, 1936; "Vendée," *Saturday Evening Post*, Dec. 5, 1936; and "Skirmish at Sartoris," *Scribner's*, April 1935. They are listed according to their order in *The Unvanquished*.

[2] The fourth, fifth, and sixth stories show little change from the magazine versions, except in occasional phrases. The first three stories have been expanded; they are about one-third longer than the original ones. Some descriptive detail has been added, but most of the changes consist of new blocks of material that do not contribute significantly to the story. For example, the new material about the McCaslins' method of sharing the land and about the combat between the two locomotives seem interesting but pointless digressions. And the attempt to make the locomotive symbolic of the Negro race's "impulse to move" seems

pares these changes with the revisions that went into the
writing of *The Hamlet* and *Go Down, Moses*—particularly
the final versions of "Spotted Horses," "The Hound,"[3] and
"Lion," where the author's imagination has seized and re-
worked the material into new and powerful works of art—
it is apparent that the stories of *The Unvanquished* kindled
little spark in Faulkner during the revisions. The explanation for this lack of imaginative reworking of the material
seems to reside in the narrowness and superficiality of the
author's approach as well as in the slightness of the material.
Compared with *Absalom*'s tragic tale of the Southern past,
this thin, sentimentalized version seems the work of another
author. Nevertheless, it does represent an aspect of Faulkner which requires further examination.

The stories revolve principally around Bayard Sartoris
and Granny Millard, a boy and an old lady; this determines,
in large part, the outlook and scope of *The Unvanquished*.
Both Bayard and Granny have their own kind of innocence:
his a boyish romanticism and naiveté, hers a simplistic piety
and loyalty. The stories are dominated by Bayard's point of
view, but they are apparently told by an older Bayard looking reminiscently back upon the innocence of his younger
days. Ignorant of the issues that have led Southerner and
Northerner into civil conflict, the boy, in "Ambuscade," plays
at war with his Negro companion, Ringo. He plays as if the
difference in the color of their skins did not matter, as if he
were holding "intact the pattern of recapitulant mimic furious victory like a cloth, a shield between ourselves and real-

---

even less successful. However, Faulkner does seem more aware of
Ringo's race in *The Unvanquished*, for he tells us twice that Ringo's
color does not matter (see pp.7-8 and 91). In *The Unvanquished*
Faulkner also establishes that the narrator is an older Bayard reminisc-
ing about his boyhood (see p.11).

[3] For commentary on the revisions of these stories, see pp. 139-140.

ity, between us and fact and doom."[4] When Loosh, a slave aware of the color of his skin, cries out, " 'Gin'ral Sherman gonter sweep the earth and the race gonter all be free!' " (25-26), the white boy innocently takes up the cry: " 'They're coming to set us free!' " (26) Later, however, white and black boys shoot at a "Yankee bastud." The Yankees have occupied the area, but no punishment ensues for the boys, because a brave grandmother hides them and a kindly Yankee colonel goes along with the deception. In a world where decency readily prevails, even in wartime, all that remains is to wash away the curse of the word "bastud." The make-believe is not entirely Bayard Sartoris'; it is William Faulkner's.

The humor that makes this sentimentalized version of the War entertaining continues in the next story, "Retreat." However, the relationship between Yankee and Southerner becomes less gracious when the Yankees seize the Sartoris mules and silver. And when the Yankees burn down the Sartoris home, the story ends with Granny too crying out against the invaders—"the bastuds!" The reader's sympathy is enlisted on the side of the Southern victims of Northern destruction, although it is distracted by Loosh's departure in the name of black freedom: " 'I going. I done been freed; God's own angel proclamated me free and gonter general me to Jordan. I don't belong to John Sartoris now; I belongs to me and God' " (85). Still, since the prevailing point of view remains that of the slaveholder, Loosh's departure is felt to be a desertion of the Sartorises in the time of their need. The story's concern for the Negro is only momentary; its chief concern is for the Sartorises.

But the intensity of the Negroes' hunger for freedom does seem to move the author. The picture that he paints of

---

[4] William Faulkner, *The Unvanquished* (New York, Random House, 1938), p.4. Page references are to this edition.

their march to freedom is one of the most powerful in the book. Caught up in a kind of religious fervor, they sweep blindly on toward their vision of the promised land. Even Granny, journeying to Alabama in pursuit of the Sartoris silver and mules, is caught in the wake of this tidal wave. Singing of the glory of their vision, the Negroes march en masse into the river. They move on despite the Yankee officer and troopers beating at them with their scabbards and despite Granny raining blows down upon them with her parasol. While the Yankees want to get on with the war, and Granny wants to get back her silver and mules and slaves, the Negroes want their promised land. But the river the Negroes have reached is not the River Jordan, and their quest for freedom, Faulkner implies, is but mass delusion and hysteria.

The protagonist of *The Unvanquished* is the slaveholder and not the slave; in most of the stories the major protagonist is Granny Millard. Although Colonel Sartoris single-handedly captures a Yankee company, Granny, with some help from Ringo, outsmarts the entire Yankee army in Mississippi. The Yankees may have taken a chest of silver and a pair of mules from her, but Granny establishes a thriving mule business wherein she sells and resells to the Yankees hundreds of mules she has got from them on forged orders. Like the clever yeoman of English legend she robs the rich to help the country poor, but unlike Robin Hood she mixes piety with shrewdness. She engages in deception reluctantly and, after the Yankees have put her out of business, she enters the church to confess to God:

"I have sinned. I have stolen, and I have borne false witness against my neighbor, though that neighbor was an enemy of my country. And more than that, I have caused these children to sin. I hereby take their sins upon my conscience. . . . But I did not sin for gain or for greed," Granny said. "I did not sin for revenge. I defy You or anyone to say I did. I sinned first for justice. And after that first time, I sinned for more than justice; I sinned for the sake of food and clothes for Your own creatures who could not help themselves—for children who had given their fathers, for wives who had given their husbands, for old people who had given their sons to a holy cause, even though You have seen fit to make it a lost cause. What I gained, I shared with them. It is true that I kept some of it back, but I am the best judge of that because I, too, have dependents who may be orphans, too, at this moment, for all I know. And if this be sin in Your sight, I take this on my conscience too. Amen." (167-68)

Amusingly, what begins as a confession of sin becomes a challenge and reproof to God. The cause which God has seen fit to make a lost one, Granny persists, is still a holy cause. Characteristically her confession breathes more defiance and assurance than remorse or repentance. It is this stubbornness—indomitability, Faulkner would say—that constitutes her chief appeal. During the four years of war "she hadn't got any older or weaker, but just littler and littler and straighter and straighter and more and more indomitable" (163). Her Christian righteousness and paternalism, pride and resistance, will and power to act are qualities that Faulkner apparently identifies with the Old South. It is Granny, rather than Colonel Sartoris, who is the true hero of *The Unvanquished;* it is feminine strength, rather than masculine power, that remains unvanquished.

But then Granny died. In the rain Brother Fortinbride and the hill people whom Granny had helped when she was alive buried her in the red earth. She had been murdered by Grumby, a cowardly marauder who attacked and robbed defenseless women and children. Induced by Ab Snopes to deal with Grumby, Granny had acted partly out of self-interest—that is, the desire to help recoup the Sartoris for-

tunes—and partly out of an innocence that was a form of
self-deception: she refused to recognize Grumby for what
he was, "because she still believed that what side of a war a
man fought on made him what he is" (170). Her death ini-
tiates the boys' unrelenting pursuit of the murderer and ends
only when the murderer's corpse is "pegged out on the door
. . . like a coon hide" (213) and his right hand is fixed to
Granny's grave-marker.

With the death of Granny, the book shifts from the War
to the Reconstruction era, from the grim mood of the boys'
pursuit of the murderer to the light, humorous tone of "Skirmish at Sartoris." There are two skirmishes—one between
Drusilla and the female paladins of Southern womanhood
and respectability over the question of Drusilla's marriage
to Colonel Sartoris, the other between the Colonel and fed-
eral officials, the Burdens, over the attempted election of
a Negro marshal. The first skirmish is regarded lightly,
for it is a foregone conclusion that the women will have their
way and men must not protest too much; this skirmish ends
good-humoredly in defeat for Drusilla. But the second is
regarded more seriously, for Colonel Sartoris kills the Burdens; and the skirmish ends, after the Negro candidate has
been voted down by the whites, in a victory by exultant
Southerners over meddling Northerners.

Despite the humor, the story's point of view is too tenden-
tiously and narrowly Southern. Never once in the story—or,
for that matter, in the entire volume—does the author truly
consider whether the Negro too may be entitled to human
rights. The "good" Negro, like Ringo, remains loyal to his
white masters and even fights for his "nigger" status. As a
boy, Ringo is considered almost one of the family; and since
the book holds on to the feeling of a boy's world, the picture
of the Negro-white relationship is essentially idyllic rather

than realistic. Like the boy in "Ambuscade" who enacts a Southern victory at the very time when Vicksburg has been lost to the North, Faulkner tries to hold intact a vision of the South that seems a half-truth—"like a cloth, a shield between ourselves and reality, between us and fact and doom" (4). For the most part, the Faulkner of *The Unvanquished* idealizes and oversimplifies the Southern past. Various Southern myths are embedded in the stories: for example, that the slave was a contented member of Southern society, that hence the South was a victim of Yankee meddling and aggression, and that the slaveholder of the Old South was generally motivated by the humane and Christian considerations of a Granny Millard and not, of course, by the self-interest of an Ab Snopes or Grumby. The stereotypes to which the author clings suggest some fundamental unwillingness to confront reality.

But in the last story, "An Odor of Verbena," Faulkner breaks through the surface and renders into life the inner struggle within the conscience of Bayard Sartoris. It is the struggle between Christian morality and a code based on violence—a central issue in the Reconstruction South. That Faulkner has been gripped by the issue and is involved in his protagonist's struggle is suggested by the story's intensity of tone, richness of symbolism, and artistry of design. "An Odor of Verbena" has the emotional involvement and moral intensity of Faulkner's best work; it merits close study.

"An Odor of Verbena" covers twenty-four hours in the life of Bayard, the only son of Colonel Sartoris. It opens in Oxford on an October evening in 1873. Bayard, twenty-four now, was studying law in his room at Professor Wilkins' house when the news of his father's murder suddenly shattered the peaceful darkness of the evening. Bayard was snatched out of his short-lived peace and flung into the crisis that he and his generation had to face in the Reconstruction South. He would have to make a choice between the Southern code, which demanded retaliation for the killing of one's kin, and the Biblical commandment against killing. "If there was anything at all in the Book, anything of hope and peace for His blind and bewildered spawn . . . *Thou shalt not kill* must be it" (249). But he could not ponder the dilemma now, for Ringo and the horses were waiting the return to Jefferson.

As he rode home toward his father's corpse, he visualized how Drusilla, his father's young wife, would receive him:

> . . . Drusilla would be waiting for me beneath all the festive glitter of the chandeliers, in the yellow ball gown and the sprig of verbena in her hair, holding the two loaded pistols (. . . I could see her, in the formal brilliant room arranged formally for obsequy, not tall, not slender as a woman is but as a youth, a boy, is, motionless, in yellow, the face calm, almost bemused, the head simple and severe, the balancing sprig of verbena above each ear, the two arms bent at the elbows, the two hands shoulder high, the two identical duelling pistols lying upon, not clutched in, one to each: the Greek amphora priestess of a succinct and formal violence). (252)

Woven into the passage is the symbolism of verbena and light that will dominate the story. The odor of verbena, invariably associated with Drusilla, would always be part of Bayard's life. Drusilla is a Roman name, verbena a sacred herb worn in ancient Roman times by the priests who served as guardians of the public faith. In "An Odor of Verbena" Drusilla represents the priestess of the Reconstruction South. She had lost her lover in the War and now she embraced, in her marriage to Colonel Sartoris, everything her husband represented: the fierce, bitter South of the nightriders who employed honor as their rallying cry, force as their method, and intolerance as their outlook. She embodied and served the "succinct and formal violence" (252) of Southern honor. Her very description—the "boy-hard body, the close implacable head with its savagely cropped hair" (257), and "the eyes staring . . . with that fierce exaltation" (270)—invests her with a savage, fanatic dedication. The light that envelops her—the light of the glittering chandeliers, the yellow ball gown, and her own brilliant eyes—suggests a feverish fire, a glittering hysteria. It is associated with the fever that plagued the unhappy South so that " 'still men must kill one another, still we must pay Cain's price in his own coin' " (246).

At midnight Bayard arrived home. It was just like a theater scene: his father's old troop waited in the background "with that curious vulture-like formality which Southern men assume in such situations" (267); Drusilla stood in the light from the open door, "emanating something louder than the two shots must have been—something voracious too and passionate" (269); he mounted the "steps toward the figure straight and yellow and immobile as a candle" (269). Then Drusilla and he were alone; it was time for the ceremony.

She faced me, she was quite near; again the scent of the verbena in her hair seemed to have increased a hundred times as she stood holding out to me, one in either hand, the two duelling pistols. "Take them, Bayard," she said, in the same tone in which she had said "Kiss me" last summer, already pressing them into my hands, watching me with that passionate and voracious exaltation, speaking in a voice fainting and passionate with promise: "Take them. I have kept them for you. I give them to you. Oh you will thank me, you will remember me who put into your hands what they say is an attribute only of God's, who took what belongs to heaven and gave it to you. Do you feel them? the long true barrels true as justice, the triggers (you have fired them) quick as retribution, the two of them slender and invincible and fatal as the physical shape of love?" (273)

The invitation to love strangely combines with the invitation to violence, as if to suggest how seductively violence proffers itself to the Southerner. The invitation to violence becomes *hybris* when Drusilla tempts Bayard to take into his own hands "what they say is an attribute only of God's" (273). Drusilla says much the same thing that Hemingway said in *Death in the Afternoon:*

> Once you accept the rule of death thou shalt not kill is an easily and naturally obeyed commandment. But when a man is still in rebellion against death he has pleasure in taking to himself one of the Godlike attributes; that of giving it. This is one of the most profound feelings in those men who enjoy killing. These things are done in pride and pride, of course, is a Christian sin and a pagan virtue.[5]

Hemingway wrote this during a period of belligerent alienation from Western civilization when he had sought in the matador's life-and-death struggle with the bull not only to shape violence into art but also to release rebellious and destructive impulses.

But Faulkner's point of view in "An Odor of Verbena" is diametrically opposed. In this story the desire to kill is depicted as a fever and hysteria; it is associated with the feverish, hysterical light of Drusilla's eyes. For Drusilla there was nothing wrong in the Colonel's shooting of two carpetbaggers; for Bayard the carpetbaggers were men, human beings (257). Killing had fed the pride and intolerance and sadism of the Colonel, until in his last days he wearied of killing men and prepared himself for "a little moral housecleaning" (266). The "instinct" that Drusilla and Hemingway would raise to a noble virtue repudiates much of our Western heritage: Greek tragedy with its profound awareness of the destructiveness inherent in man's pride, the Old Testament with its anguished faith in a just God, and the forgiveness that Christ pitted against man's vengefulness.

---

[5] Ernest Hemingway, *Death in the Afternoon* (New York, Scribner's, 1932), p. 233.

Now it was morning. The sun was nearing the hour of
Bayard Sartoris' appointment for violence. Its fierce light
seemed to replace the feverish light of Drusilla's eyes. In the
sun's savage heat and light Bayard walked to the office of
Redmond, the man who had shot his father.

It was almost noon now and I could smell nothing except the verbena in my coat, as if it had gathered all the sun, all the suspended fierce heat in which the equinox could not seem to occur
and were distilling it so that I moved in a cloud of verbena. . . .
(283)

He refused the pistol of the shocked George Wyatt, one of
his father's old troop, and alone, "enclosed in the now fierce
odor of the verbena" (285), he walked steadily on in the hot
sun. Mounting the stairs, he opened the door to walk un-
armed and dreamlike into the two orange flashes that
bloomed suddenly from Redmond's gun. Then Redmond ran
out, out of the room, out of the town forever. Bayard left
the office and "the hard fierce sun" (290), and rode to the
shaded creek bottom of the Sartoris pasture. There in the
cool shade he slept. When he awakened, the sun was gone;
there was only last night's moon. He walked back to the
house that held the corpse and dream of his father. Drusilla
was gone, but the odor of verbena remained.

The story has passed through the cycle of Bayard's crisis:
from its sudden inception that evening at Oxford twenty-four
hours earlier, to the apex of its violence at high noon in Redmond's office, to the peace of another evening. Enveloped
by the sun and odor of verbena, pierced by Drusilla's brilliant eyes and George Wyatt's "pale outraged eyes" (284),
Bayard had walked his lonely course to a Christlike deed of
nonviolence, and had passed through the day's fury to the
night's quiet. Respite will come to "this land of violent sun"
(269), Faulkner implies, only when the South, like Bayard,

has suffered a moral rebirth. Through Faulkner's recurrent use of the equinox, the story produces the effect of a delayed, laboring birth. At the opening of the story Bayard rode from Oxford "into the hot thick dusty darkness quick and strained for the overdue equinox like a laboring delayed woman" (246). When Drusilla broke into hysteria at Bayard's repudiation of the pistols, Bayard panted for breath "as though there were not enough air . . . anywhere under the heavy hot low sky where the equinox couldn't seem to accomplish" (276). When Bayard walked in the fierce sun and oppressive cloud of verbena to Redmond's office, "the equinox could not seem to occur" (283). The autumnal equinox is the harbinger of the season when the land may rest from its summer's labors and renew itself for another spring. That the equinox never occurs in "An Odor of Verbena" suggests that the South is not yet ready for renewal. One Christian act of nonviolence cannot put out the bright sun of Southern violence. The last words of the story point to the sprig of Drusilla's verbena "filling the room, the dusk, the evening with that odor which she said you could smell alone above the smell of horses" (293).

The story is centered on the inner conflict within Bayard as he struggles toward moral independence in the face of an almost hysteric social pressure. That Bayard has found it hard to breathe throughout most of the story's action suggests the sense of oppression that the South lays upon the dissenter. Whenever tension has been generated in the clash between the Southern code and his own conscience, Bayard pants for breath. His father's body laid out in regimentals, Redmond's shots, Drusilla's hysteria when he refuses the pistols, and Wyatt's shock when he refuses the gun seem to consume the very air, as if the code they represent threatens to deprive Bayard of the right to exist in the South on his own terms, as if the code equates dissent with betrayal.

Yet the feeling of disseverance only partly explains Bayard's situation. After all, he was a Southerner who wanted the good opinion of his people and who was drawn to the code he had accepted as a boy but was rejecting as a man. That Bayard has identified the code with the passionate Drusilla suggests the power and threat of its allure. Her attraction for Bayard was passionate, incestuous, and voracious. The woman his father had married after the Civil War was a product of the War; "dark, passionate and damned forever of all peace" (274), she embodies the new spirit of vengeance, violence, and hysteria. But there were other women in Bayard's life: Granny, dead now; Mrs. Wilkins, who reminded him of Granny, with her "anxious still face which was thinking [when she heard the news of the Colonel's murder] *Who lives by the sword shall die by it*" (246); and Aunt Jenny—maternal, sensible, calm, with the "same eyes as Father's except that they were intent and very wise instead of intolerant" (271). Put away the sword, put away false pride and heroics—they seemed to be telling him.

"An Odor of Verbena" reflects another point of view from that of the first six stories of *The Unvanquished*. It is a point of view characterized not by nostalgia and self-justification but by moral dissent, not by narrow pride and blind loyalty but a struggling conscience. Although the latter view is the one generally found in Faulkner's best work, both views seem to have existed in an uneasy tension within the same author. The clash of these views contributed to the making of *Absalom;* the separation of these views contributed to the making of *The Unvanquished.*

Yet the character of Bayard Sartoris marks a significant stage in the evolution of the Faulkner hero. Ten years earlier in *The Sound and the Fury* the Faulkner hero chose death as an answer to his dilemma. Now in "An Odor of Verbena" another idealistic young man faces a different but similar dilemma. Both young men were involved in incestuous love: Quentin could not give up the sister he identified with a lost honor; Bayard repudiated his stepmother for another ideal. Quentin's idealism turned backward to self and downward to death; Bayard's idealism turned from the Southern code to Christian pacifism. Bayard is the bridge between Quentin Compson and Isaac McCaslin. He marks a stage in the journey of the Faulkner hero from Quentin's destructive guilt to Isaac's social conscience, from death to life.

8

The Wild Palms

When *The Wild Palms* first appeared in 1939, it puzzled and irritated reviewers. Different from most of Faulkner's other novels in its characters, milieu, and subject, it represented a departure for the author from the familiar world of Yoknapatawpha to the strange middle-class world of New Orleans and Chicago. The reviewers' objections centered, however, not on Faulkner's new subject matter but on his new technique. The joining of two apparently unrelated stories, "Wild Palms" and "Old Man," in alternating chapters seemed to them a meaningless contrivance or, at best, a Faulknerian joke. When Malcolm Cowley, rejecting Faulkner's arrangement and discarding the "Wild Palms" story as inferior, published "Old Man" separately in *The Portable Faulkner* (1946), he seemed to be expressing the accepted view. Later separate Signet editions of the two stories[1] reinforced the impression that Faulkner's arrangement was best forgotten.

One of the first critics to question this view was Irving

[1] *The Wild Palms* (New York, New American Library, 1948) and *The Old Man* (New York, New American Library, 1948). In 1954 the two stories were printed together by New American Library but without the alternation of the chapters.

Howe. Noting various correspondences and oppositions between the two stories, he implied that the two parts are
"bound together by theme and atmosphere" and that taken
together the two stories "might yield a tone of dissonant irony
which neither could alone."[2] Later critics have stressed or
discovered other correspondences and antitheses,[3] but they
generally accept the view that the stories are united, though
not necessarily successfully, by a counterpoint of theme and
atmosphere.

The counterpoint, according to Faulkner, grew naturally
out of the writing of the book:

> To tell the story I wanted to tell, which was the one of the in-
> tern and the woman who gave up her family and husband to run
> off with him. To tell it like that, somehow or another I had to
> discover counterpoint for it, so I invented the other story, its
> complete antithesis, to use as counterpoint. And I did not write
> those two stories and then cut one into the other. I wrote them
> as you read it, as the chapters. The chapter of the *Wild Palms*,
> chapter of the *River Story*, another chapter of the *Wild Palms*,
> and then I used the counterpoint of another chapter of the *River
> Story*. I imagined as a musician would do to compose a piece of
> music in which he needed a balance, a counterpoint.[4]

---

[2] Irving Howe, *William Faulkner: A Critical Study*, pp.172 and 177.

[3] The best recent criticism of *The Wild Palms* is the article by Joseph
J. Moldenhauer, "Unity of Theme and Structure in *The Wild Palms*,"
in Frederick J. Hoffman and Olga W. Vickery (eds.), *William Faulkner:
Three Decades of Criticism*, pp.305-322. See also Hyatt H. Waggoner,
William Faulkner: From Jefferson to the World, pp.132-147; Olga W.
Vickery, *The Novels of William Faulkner*, pp.156-166; W. R. Moses,
"The Unity of *The Wild Palms*," *Modern Fiction Studies*, 2 (Autumn,
1956), 125-131, and "Water, Water Everywhere: *Old Man* and *A
Farewell to Arms*," *Modern Fiction Studies*, 5 (Summer, 1959), 172-
174; and H. Edward Richardson, "The 'Hemingwaves' in Faulkner's
The Wild Palms," *Modern Fiction Studies*, 4 (Winter, 1958-1959),
357-360.

[4] *Faulkner at Nagano*, ed. Robert A. Jelliffe (Tokyo, Kenkyusha
Press, 1956), pp.79-80. See also Jean Stein, "William Faulkner: An
Interview," in *William Faulkner: Three Decades of Criticism*, pp.75-76,
and Gwynn and Blotner (eds.), *Faulkner in the University*, pp.8, 72-73,
and 171-184.

The alternating of the stories' chapters is based largely, then, on the author's intuitive awareness of the need to change the mood and setting, to change the story itself. Faulkner did somewhat the same thing in *The Sound and the Fury* when he moved abruptly from the neurosis and idealism of the Quentin section to the comedy and materialism of the Jason section—the comedy providing relief, the materialism depicting the kind of world Quentin had fled. Not only does the humor of the "Old Man" provide some relief from the depressiveness of the Wilbourne story, but the character of the tall convict, by its very difference, comments on the nature of Harry Wilbourne. As the book shuttles back and forth between the two stories, it imposes on the reader an increasing awareness of contrast. It is the sharp, ironic contrast between two worlds, two men, and two loves.

One is the world of the River, the Old Man: the "strong brown god—sullen, untamed and intractable . . . almost forgotten by the dwellers in cities."[5] Its crest swirling "like the mane of a galloping horse,"[6] the River reared and leaped over man's puny dikes and pushed with ruthless male force over the face of the land. Caught in the midst of such force, man was like an insect helpless and ignorant of the power of nature that worked outside and within him. Yet when the Old Man snatched up the tall convict, the convict fought back, pitting his blood and strength against the Old Man's savage power in the same instinctive way that primitive man might have struggled for survival. "Old Man" is the story of that struggle—a fine and natural struggle, Faulkner seems to say—for which a man must have preserved something of

---

[5] T. S. Eliot, "The Dry Salvages," *Four Quartets* (New York, Harcourt, Brace, 1943), p.21.

[6] William Faulkner, *The Wild Palms* (New York, Random House, 1939), p.156. This edition will be used for all quotations from the novel.

the strength and simplicity of another time. In the novel's opposition between nature and civilization, the convict, stemming from some "dim hill-bred Abraham" (255), is natural man. Imprisoned by society for having been seduced by its novels about the Diamond Dicks and Jesse Jameses, the hillbilly had chosen to work on the penal farm. There, as year followed year, he plowed the rich black earth with the mule he called John Henry. A simple Southern backwoodsman, he even refused promotion to trusty because he preferred the earth to the trusty's gun.

In the world of the tall convict, the pregnant woman, and the Old Man, we are isolated from civilization and caught up in a liberating struggle between man and nature. Although marked by violence and the convict's amusingly frenzied need to rid himself of the woman, this world is an idyllic one, cut off from civilization's time and receding into the dim past. There is the stirring birth scene upon the ancient Indian mound, just a bit of land in a sea of water, an "earthen Ark out of Genesis" (232). In the midst of the wild animals seeking refuge from the flood, the convict assisted the woman in delivering the child. After the birth, he made fire and cooked a rabbit he had taken from a hawk. He fed the woman; then, both having eaten, they slept beside the fire in the peaceful interlaced gloom of the cypresses. Like Noah and his family, they seem God's chosen. Later in their odyssey they seem to be carried back to some primordial time when the earth was but swampland inhabited by saurian monsters and inarticulate savages. This was the interlude when they lived with the Cajan, and when the convict, with knife and club, fought his bloody battles with thrashing alligators. For the convict this was the good life.

He lived with the woman for seven weeks on the Mississippi. Her pregnancy and later the newborn child invested her with such inviolability that, instinctively, he avoided sexual relations with her: "his whole being would seem to flee the very idea in a kind of savage and horrified revulsion" (335). He lived only as protector and provider, she as mother; together they were like a primitive family. This family seems symbolic of life itself, the very image of the three within the shell of the boat enclosed by water suggesting a universal symbol of birth.

The tall convict is another of Faulkner's hillmen—stoic, naive, uncomplicated, desiring little in life. In the face of a "niggard fate of hard and unceasing travail" (256) and a partly comical series of disasters, he endures and prevails. Paradoxically he is characterized by independence, for his power and will to act have not been vitiated by civilization; in this sense he is a free man. Rejected by society during the long journey down the Mississippi, he made his way back to return the woman, the skiff, and himself to the authorities at the exact spot where the flood had first snatched him up. His journey had never become flight. His simple and absolute integrity shines like a lonely light in the midst of the political corruption and chicanery of his jailers.

But the intertwining of the stories' chapters constantly reminds us that another world rules, the world that has imprisoned the natural man. It is the middle-class world of Charlotte Rittenmeyer, the "liberated" woman who has abandoned the role of mother and wife and who has, by default, taken over the role of the male; it is the world of Harry Wilbourne, the helpless modern male marked for defeat by a stasis of will and failure of nerve; and it is the world of Rat Rittenmeyer, the cuckolded husband, whose masculinity has been clipped by the conformist pressures and inhibited emotions of his upper middle-class society. Particularly in the relationships that unite the male with the female protagonists

of each story—what Faulkner has called "two types of love"[7]
—are the differences of these two worlds highlighted.

The tall convict and the pregnant woman had not chosen
each other; they were held together by circumstance. The
convict wanted, most of all, to get rid of her, but to get rid
of her in the right way. She was, by his simple hillman's code,
his responsibility. Yet they were united not merely by circumstance and his sense of duty but by their common hillfolk
heritage and by the mutual crises they had endured. Theirs
was the rapport conferred upon them

by the two weeks during which they had jointly suffered all the
crises emotional social economic and even moral which do not
always occur even in the ordinary fifty married years (the old
married: you have seen them, the electroplate reproductions, the
thousand identical coupled faces with only a collarless stud or
a fichu out of Louisa Alcott to denote the sex, looking in pairs
like the winning braces of dogs after a field trial, out from among
the packed columns of disaster and alarm and baseless assurance
and hope and incredible insensitivity and insulation from tomorrow propped by a thousand morning sugar bowls or coffee urns.
(254)

But the love that bound Wilbourne and Charlotte is an
altogether different affair; it is significantly involved with our
middle-class society. Part of the revolt against bourgeois respectability and convention, this passion combines Byronic
rebellion with romantic exaltation of love. Stemming from
the Romantic protest against the nineteenth-century bour-
geoisie and the Industrial Revolution, this type of love has
found apt expression in the dreams and yearnings of Flau-
bert's Madame Bovary. The twentieth century, however, in
loosening the moorings of traditional morality, not only pro-

---

[7] Lavon Roscoe, "An Interview with William Faulkner," *Western
Review*, 15 (Summer, 1951), 300.

vided the novelist with more liberty, but also changed the quality of the love; it lessened its sublimation but intensified the glorification of its physical aspect. One of its best literary exponents is Ernest Hemingway. In his novels Hemingway has centered love in physical passion, darkened it with doom, and projected society as its enemy. It is this concept of love that Faulkner has made part of the thesis of *The Wild Palms,* though, unlike Hemingway, he has not identified uncritically with the lovers. The difference in the authors' point of view modifies the meaning and value of the love. In *A Farewell to Arms* society offends against love; in *The Wild Palms* love offends against society.

The relationship between the convict and the pregnant woman derives from their roles in the family unit; since their individuality is subordinated to family life, they are nameless representatives of Man and Woman. The relationship between Charlotte Rittenmeyer and Harry Wilbourne derives from the delusions and discontent of middle-class society, and is a form of romantic individualism destructive of society. The convict and the pregnant woman lived in instinctual rapport with nature, but Charlotte and Harry lived in an ugly alienation from nature. The flight of Charlotte and Harry is characterized by the unnatural, destructive, and moribund aspects of their lives and surroundings. It is a flight from the traditional roles of man and woman; it is a flight from life.

In Chicago—with its streets like "stone canyons" (119), its "corpse- and hell-glowing" (96) neon lights, its "hearse-like limousines" (97)—Charlotte's strong, supple hands supported the two of them. She made grotesque figurines out of wire and paper, while Harry sat on a park bench and brooded obsessively on the dwindling bank balance. Their retreat to a Wisconsin lake did not establish any rapport between the lovers and nature. While she swam and sunned herself, he slumbered in "a drowsy and foetuslike state" (110) or compulsively counted and recounted the diminishing cans of their food. On their return to Chicago, their existence became still more bizarre and inverted: each worked while the other slept. At night she worked amid the "jointless figures with suave organless bodies and serene almost incredible faces" (120) of manikins; during the day he wrote trashy confessional stories that began with " 'I had the body and desires of a woman yet in knowledge and experience of the world I was but a child' or 'If I had only had a mother's love to guard me on that fatal day' " (121). To escape their unnatural, loveless routine, the lovers fled to the frozen inferno of a Utah mine that defaced nature and exploited man. Ironically it was in this bleak, cold retreat that Charlotte, waiting in vain for the spring that was never to come, first felt the stirrings of life within her womb. But for the lovers this life signified only love's barrier and threat. They fled in panic back to civilization, where the doctor sought ineffectually from druggists and a brothel-keeper the means to kill the unborn child. Unable to abort the child and wearied to death by bitter quarrels, they fled southward to New Orleans and the Mississippi coast, back to the shabby scaling palms, back to the birthplace of their deteriorating love. Here, in the rented beach cottage of a small seacoast village, the lovers' flight was to end.

This final scene dominates the novel. It opens the novel and closes the "Wild Palms" story. The setting is the squalid cottage murmurous with the ghosts of sordid lusts. Its landlord-panderers are a middle-aged provincial doctor and his gray, gorgonlike wife, who are joined in sterile union and walled behind Baptist righteousness; theirs was a life Wilbourne might have fallen into, had he not cast his lot with romantic love. Outside the cottage, a black wind of death blew in from the sea over the dark sand and through the dry clashing palms; it whispered and murmured and filled the cottage with its presence. Inside the cottage with its smell of cold, stale gumbo on a cold stove,[8] Charlotte thrashed with pain, while her lover watched helplessly. Pervading the scene is a sense of covert shame and impending disaster; the dominant symbols are blood, the wind, and the wild palms. The "thread of blood" along Charlotte's mouth and the blood dripping from her womb signify not birth and life, as with the convict's woman, but abortion and death. The wild palms seem associated both with the memory of Charlotte and Harry thrashing in love and with the present reality of Charlotte thrashing in the throes of death. Their love sought a passionate sterility but has found only death. The increasing murmur of the wind in the palms suggests first the presage of death, then the presence of death, and finally, as Wilbourne sat in his prison cell, the memory of death. Like the River, the wind seems to mock at man's futile attempts to thwart nature.

The love of Charlotte and Harry has carried its own seeds of death. Denying the parental role and necessitating aborticide, their love is ultimately destructive of themselves and the race. Such a love signifies a suicidal force of civilization. Its counterpoint is found, of course, in the story of the convict and the woman who live in rapport with nature. The novel's title suggests other variations on the opposition between civilization and nature. The wild palms are also hands: the inept hands of Wilbourne and the wildly amorous hands of Charlotte. Wilbourne's hands open tin cans, type trashy stories, and kill his woman and child; but the tall convict's hands till the soil, fashion tools, kill to provide food, and de-

---

[8] In *The Sound and the Fury* the cold stove to which Dilsey returned after the Easter service was part of the decaying house where family love had died and Christ had not been resurrected.

liver a child. Their hands are symbols, respectively, of civilized and primitive societies. Wilbourne represents the emasculated middle-class male whose education has proved unavailing for life's crises; he is helpless. The representative of civilization is characterized by indecision and introversion, the primitive by deeds. The "Wild Palms" story is oppressed by lifelessness and frustration; the "Old Man" story is liberated by movement and action.

The depressiveness of "Wild Palms" resides chiefly not in the defeat of the lovers but in the author's failure to accord emotion and life to their love. The failure seems bound up with the author's underlying antagonism to what he was trying to create. The antagonism, partly rationalized in the novel's thesis that civilization is alienated from nature, seems to stem ultimately from the abhorrence of sex that dominated the Quentin section of *The Sound and the Fury* and that left its mark upon *Sanctuary* and *Light in August*. The drowning-image which reflected that antagonism persists in *The Wild Palms* and suggests that woman still threatens to engulf man. Wilbourne described the loss of virginity as a lonely terror-stricken ride over a dark precipice down to a kind of death by drowning: " 'the darkness, the falling, the thunder of solitude, the shock, the death, the moment when, stopped physically by the ponderable clay, you yet feel all your life rush out of you into the pervading immemorial blind receptive matrix, the hot fluid blind formation—grave-womb or womb-grave, it's all one' " (138). When Wilbourne fell in love, "he seemed to be drowning, volition and will, in the yellow stare" (39), "the unwinking yellow stare in which he seemed to blunder and fumble like a moth, a rabbit caught in the glare of a torch; an envelopment almost like a liquid" (87).

This feeling of suppressed antagonism seems part of Wilbourne's prolonged virginity. Yet—unlike Quentin Compson, who identified the honor of his family with the chastity of his sister—Wilbourne attributed much of his problem to his virginity: "'I waited too long; twenty-seven is too long to wait to get out of your system what you should have rid yourself of at fourteen or fifteen or maybe even younger'" (137). In his relationship with Charlotte he was like a dependent child: "'maybe I'm not embracing her but clinging to her,'" he admitted, "'because there is something in me that wont admit it cant swim'" (84). In their lovemaking he was the compliant but reluctant victim, she the aggressor. She brought to their love the strength and courage he lacked; she proved to be a better man than he. But in the last days of her life she seemed to turn against the whole race of man, as if she knew how badly her lover had failed her. Fundamentally "Wild Palms" is the story not of Wilbourne's love but of his struggle with love.[9] In his attempt to become her lover, he was struggling against what he wanted to want. He was not at ease until Charlotte was dead and he was alone with his grief.

The love between Charlotte and Harry possesses neither joy nor tenderness, because the author, like the protagonist of "Wild Palms," seems imprisoned in a reluctant puritanism. This ambivalence is apparent too in the author's romantic and anti-romantic outlook. At the same time that he portrays

---

[9] Moldenhauer has suggested that "the same Puritan preoccupation with a fixed moral and social order which has molded the doctor [the provincial doctor who rented the cottage to Wilbourne] lies behind Wilbourne's incapacity to enjoy the pagan freedom Charlotte offers him, behind his masochistic and self-defeating efforts to refute that order, and behind his final eager acceptance of the sentence pronounced by an outraged gulf-town court. Fearful of physical love and unable to escape or obey his conscience, Harry Wilbourne follows a course of frenzied self-punishment which culminates in his blundering and compulsive murder of Charlotte" (*William Faulkner: Three Decades of Criticism*, p.309). Moldenhauer's emphasis on puritanism seems correct, but at times it is not entirely clear whether the puritanism in "Wild Palms" is intended or is an unconscious projection of the author.

Charlotte's and Harry's love as "the passionate idea of two damned and doomed and isolated forever against the world and God" (82), he says that "love no more exists just at one spot and in one moment and in one body out of all the earth and all time and all the teeming breathed, than sunlight does" (43). It is only when Faulkner moves into the world of the tall convict and the pregnant woman that he seems truly at home, for this is a world where man is naturally exempt from the need to make love.[10] Both comic and moving, the "Old Man" releases the curious frustrations of "Wild Palms" and lifts us into a world where man has the strength of simplicity and where woman fulfills her traditional role.

What emerges from "Wild Palms" is neither a credible love relationship nor a convincing society. Basically the society seems the kind of stereotyped image of the middle class that a hostile and alien mind might conceive. The author has not truly succeeded in rendering into life his critical view of our modern world. As a result, the novel fails, but it fails most interestingly. One must admit too that the novel fails because the counterpoint is not integrated organically into the novel's structure; alternating the stories' chapters is a mechanical, inartistic device for establishing counterpoint. Nevertheless, the thesis of *The Wild Palms*—that civilization is suicidally alienated from nature—apparently stemmed from one of Faulkner's most deep-rooted convictions, for it would provide the basis for "The Bear" and, in later years, for *A Fable*.

---

10 After the "Old Man" story, Faulkner's protagonists in his works of the 1940's are usually boys, old men, or natural bachelors—Ratliff, Sam Fathers, Isaac McCaslin, Chuck Mallison, Lucas Beauchamp, and Gavin Stevens. With the exception of Isaac in the brief scene depicting his rejection of his wife, these protagonists are insulated from sexual problems.

9

The Hamlet

In the writing of *The Hamlet* (1940), Faulkner continued the tendency, apparent in *The Unvanquished* and *The Wild Palms,* to fashion a single work out of a group of related stories. Much of the material for this work he found in stories he had written years ago.[1] Three of these stories—

---

[1] According to Faulkner, he wrote the stories in the late twenties and pulled them together in 1940 (see *Faulkner in the University,* pp. 14-15); these stories probably include all but "Barn Burning." They were first published as follows: "Spotted Horses," *Scribner's,* 89 (June 1931), 585-597; "The Hound," *Harper's,* 163 (Aug. 1931), 266-274; "Lizards in Jamshyd's Courtyard," *Saturday Evening Post,* 204 (Feb. 27, 1932), 12-13, 52, 57; "Fool About a Horse," *Scribner's,* 100 (Aug. 1936), 80-86; "Barn Burning," *Harper's,* 179 (June 1939), 86-96. In adapting these stories to *The Hamlet,* Faulkner did most of his rewriting on "The Hound" (the Houston murder story) and "The Spotted Horses" (the horse auction), revised "Fool About a Horse" (story of the horse swap) least of all, and used only part of "Barn Burning" (eliminating the role of the boy, Colonel Sartoris Snopes). "Lizards in Jamshyd's Courtyard" (the treasure hunt story) he expanded in detail, but except for the introduction of Lump Snopes and the change of Suratt to Ratliff, he did not change the basic plot. In expanding "The Hound" and "The Spotted Horses" to about three times their original length, he deepened their meaning and heightened their power. Generally he tried to elevate the language and "universalize" the imagery; that is, to reduce the dialectalisms and folkishness. See Peter Lisca, "*The Hamlet:* Genesis and Revisions," *Faulkner Studies,* 3 (Spring 1954), 5-13; and Floyd C. Watkins and Thomas Daniel Young, "Revisions of Style in Faulkner's *The Hamlet,*" *Modern Fiction Studies,* 5 (Winter 1959-1960), 327-336.

"Spotted Horses," "Lizards in Jamshyd's Courtyard," and
"Fool About a Horse"—were in the backwoods tradition of
the tall tale and folk humor, their subject the battle of wits
between the shrewd trader and his rivals. Two other stories,
"Barn Burning" and "The Hound," dealt with more grim and
poignant aspects of the life of the small farmer in the Deep
South and provided material for the portraits of Ab and Mink
Snopes. The stories of the strange loves of Labove and Eula
Varner, Jack Houston and Lucy Pate, Mink Snopes and the
nymphomaniac, and the idiot and the cow were new material.[2] Old and new material—no matter how variegated in
theme, tone, and genre—Faulkner sought to fuse into a single
work of art. Whether and how he succeeded have been the
subject of critical debate.

Three critical views seem to dominate: (1) that *The Hamlet* is not a novel but a series of loosely connected episodes,[3]
(2) that it is a novel unified by the theme of the Snopeses'
demoralization of Frenchman's Bend,[4] and (3) that its meaning is centered in the successive stories of barter and love.[5]

---

[2] The story about the idiot and the cow is not entirely new, since it
partly derives from the burlesque parody entitled "Afternoon of a Cow"
(translated into French by Professor Coindreau and published in
Fontaine, 27-28 [June-July 1943], 66-81; printed in English in *Furioso*,
2 [Summer 1947], 5-17; manuscript presented by Faulkner to Professor
Coindreau in 1937). However, there is neither an idiot nor an account
of a romance with a cow in "Afternoon of a Cow"; hence the story in
this respect may be considered new material.

[3] Malcolm Cowley, *The Portable Faulkner*, p.366; and William Van
O'Connor, *The Tangled Fire of William Faulkner*, p.124.

[4] Irving Howe, *William Faulkner: A Critical Study*, pp.180-181;
and Viola Hopkins, "Meaning and Form in Faulkner's *The Hamlet*,"
Accent, 15 (Spring 1955), 126-127.

[5] Olga W. Vickery, *The Novels of William Faulkner*, p.167; Paul
Levine, "Love and Money in the Snopes Trilogy," *College English*, 23
(Dec. 1961), 196-199; and Norman J. Farmer, "The Love Theme: A
Principal Source of Thematic Unity in Faulkner's Snopes Trilogy,"
Twentieth Century Literature, 8 (Oct. 1962-Jan. 1963), 111-123.

If one considers *The Hamlet* as straight narrative, its disunity is obvious; but as in many of Faulkner's long works, unity is based largely on theme. Certainly the Snopes theme, closely identified with the barter theme, pulls together many of the episodes: the horse swap, the barn burning, the sale of the spotted horses, and the treasure hunt. *The Hamlet* begins with the coming of Flem Snopes and his family to French-man's Bend as unwelcome sharecroppers and ends with his triumphant departure as the new economic power of the region. Yet one must concede that Flem plays little or no part in the stories of Labove's obsessional passion for Eula Varner, the development and seduction of Eula, the romance of the idiot and the cow, the feud between Jack Houston and Lucy Pate, and Mink Snopes's murder of Jack Houston. These stories, which constitute Books Two and Three, occupy literally the center of the novel; they are generally uninflu-enced by the Snopes theme[6] and are at variance with the humor that prevails in the tales of barter. They emit another tone—intense, tortured and strange—and suggest that a dark-ness underlies the novel's comic mood. Intermittently, how-ever, comedy breaks through the somber drama to fuse dis-tress with laughter, pathos with violence, and despair with hilarity. The result is a unique counterpoint that combines diverse elements into a kind of whole.

---

[6] The significance of the Snopes theme has been generally overstated by critics. Still more objectionable is the critical stereotype that equates Snopes with animalism, amorality, and blind self-interest. Faulkner's attitude to the Snopeses is not that simple in *The Hamlet*. For example, Ab and Mink Snopes are essentially different from Flem because their lives are founded on thwarted pride, not on self-interest. Moreover the stories in which Ab and Mink play a major part, the horseswap and the Houston murder, were written originally without any Snopeses; in the revisions Faulkner changed Pap to Ab, and Ernest Cotton to Mink. Such Snopeses as Ike, Eck, and Wall are of course entirely different from Flem; in fact, they are sympathetic characters.

The subject of the work is the hamlet—the people of Frenchman's Bend. Their creation is Faulkner's great achievement in this novel. His rendering of a scene, an act, a face or gesture often flashes a light into the nature of a character and the community, so that the image becomes a glimpse into a specific condition and a way of life. It is hard to forget the scene where Mink's wife and children, on the night he returns from the murder, take their few belongings and leave him alone in the empty cabin, the older child hurrying back to clasp to its breast "a wooden block with the tops of four snuff tins nailed to it like wheels" (255)[7] and then going on into the dark to join the mother; or the scene where Mrs. Armstid—gaunt in a shapeless gray garment, her hands rolled in her apron, her eyes cast down, her voice toneless—asks Flem for the five dollars, while the men on the gallery look away; or the image of her husband digging madly for money, digging on "into the waxing twilight with the regularity of a mechanical toy and with something monstrous in his unflagging effort" (419). There is no end to what one may remember about these people. *The Hamlet* is their story—the story of their passions, rancors, greed, and violence; the story of their decency, kindliness, shrewdness, and wry humor. The chief commentator on their antics and foibles is Ratliff, who serves like the chorus of ancient drama to give voice to the community's sanity and conscience. It is his ironic humor, as well as Will Varner's, that provides the novel with its perspective and tone.

The novel begins with a brief survey of the people's origins: the migrations of their ancestors from England and Scotland and Wales to the Atlantic seaboard and thence, by stages, through the Tennessee mountains to Mississippi; the

---

[7] Page references to *The Hamlet* are from the Random House (1940) edition.

displacement of the planter and his slaves by these indepen-
dent settlers, of the plantation house and the slave quarters
by the unpainted cabins, and, in time, of the great fields by
the "small shiftless mortgaged farms for the directors of
Jefferson banks to squabble over before selling finally to Will
Varner" (4). The shift of the economic and political power
of Frenchman's Bend from the planter to Varner was part
of an historical process which the novelist does not question;
as for Will Varner himself, Faulkner apparently likes him,
likes his shrewdness and earthy realism. Shrewdness, in fact,
is the subject of Book One and the basis for its comedy.

The action begins with the coming of Ab Snopes. His stiff
heavy limp across the porch of Varner's store, when he departed for the farm he had just rented from Jody Varner on
shares, had an element of threat, as if the limp were Ab's
constant reminder of the grudge he bore the gentry and the
world.[8] But the threat had little effect on Jody at first, as he
planned to use Ab's reputation as a barnburner to cheat Ab
out of his share of the crop. When Ratliff told Jody how
quickly Ab took offense and how still more quickly he burned
barns, the conniver changed to victim: the trickster had out-
foxed himself. The comedy rests not only on the change but
on the contrast between the storyteller's blandness and the
listener's apoplectic horror, Jody's "hell fire" punctuating the
story like a comic refrain. By the time the frightened Jody
rides off to placate the barnburners and ends by trading Ab's
son a clerkship in the store for unguaranteed fire insurance,

---

[8] Ab's grudge is directed against the gentry because they have shot
him. There are two versions of the shooting: (1) that Colonel Sartoris
shot Ab in the heel when he tried to steal the Colonel's stallion during
the War (p.19); (2) that a provost's man shot Ab in the heel on a
stolen horse (see "Barn Burning" in *Collected Stories,* p.5, and *The
Hamlet,* p.33). Regardless of the difference in the versions, for Ab the
ruling class has injured him.

Jody's horror has changed to desperate volubility, and the comedy mounts in a gleeful crescendo. The comic contrast between Jody's state of mind and the others' is nicely sustained, the characterization is deft, the talk and the silences are superb.

The comedy continues in the tale of the horse swap. It is based on the contrast between Pat Stamper's wily artistry and Ab Snopes's growing frustration. In the horsetraders' battle of wits, Ab is not Stamper's match, for his country shrewdness cannot compete with the other's genius. Although narrated by Ratliff as a sympathetic reminiscence of Ab, the story belongs to Stamper. It has such a candid boy's delight in the legerdemain of the master horsetrader that Stamper becomes the hero. In humor and language Faulkner's tale seems close to *Huckleberry Finn*. It is told in the simple dialectal language and vivid homespun imagery of a Huck and has Huck's feeling of compassion for the underdog.[9] It shows too the humorist's fondness for a funny though irrelevant story, for the story does not really explain, as Ratliff claims, why Ab became curdled. But it does not have to; it is the right kind of comedy for *The Hamlet*.

In the third chapter of Book One Faulkner shifts his emphasis, however, from Ab to Flem, from comic anecdotes to a seriocomic theme: the rise of Flem Snopes. Shrewd trading leads to more serious ramifications when the poor white's sullen grudge against the world becomes in the next generation, for someone like Flem, a singleminded acquisitiveness that knows no restraint. This acquisitiveness is different from Ratliff's desire for gain, since the sewing machine agent's pleasure in shrewd deals "transcended mere gross profit"

---

[9] In the original story, "Fool About a Horse," the narrator is a twelve-year-old boy remembering a tale about Pap. Since Faulkner's adaptation for *The Hamlet* follows the original rather closely, it retains this Huck Finn quality.

(77); and it is different from Will Varner's acquisitiveness, which was tempered by sixty years of age, an easy-going cheerful nature, common sense, and a feeling for the community. Flem's desire for money and land is more ruthless. Hence his rise to power would become a matter of concern for the community; and Ratliff, its self-appointed champion, would eventually have to do battle with him. Yet, despite the imminence of the struggle and the reality of Flem's threat, the story of his success is partly comic. Ratliff's good humor, as well as the author's own sense of amusement, hold sway.

This seriocomic quality is evident in the very description of Flem:

a thick squat soft man of no establishable age between twenty and thirty, with a broad still face containing a tight seam of mouth stained slightly at the corners with tobacco, and eyes the color of stagnant water, and projecting from among the other features in startling and sudden paradox, a tiny predatory nose like the beak of a small hawk. It was as though the original nose had been left off by the original designer or craftsman and the unfinished job taken over by someone of a radically different school or perhaps by some viciously maniacal humorist or perhaps by one who had had only time to clap into the center of the face a frantic and desperate warning. (59)

The same quality is evident too in the account of his early doings: his imitation of Jody in his wearing of white shirts[10] and of Will in his wearing of small black bowties, his challenging of Will Varner to pay five cents for the tobacco he took, and his refusal to give credit to a customer who had

---

[10] The soiled new white shirts that Flem wears for a week before discarding proclaim the new way of life he has adopted—the store for the sharecropper's farm—and suggest too a certain slovenliness and obsession with newness that Faulkner associates with people who know neither the gracious wealth of the gentry nor the decent cleanliness of the poor. One might contrast Ratliff's clean faded blue shirt with Flem's, or in *Sanctuary* the clean faded garments of Ruby Lamar with the dirty white suit of Clarence Snopes.

been in and out of the store's debt for the last fifteen years. But matters became more serious, at least for Jody, when Flem took over his job of supervising the gin while Jody went back to tending store, when Flem accompanied Will Varner in the yearly settlements of rents and debts, and when Flem became in his own right speculator, proprietor, creditor, and entrepreneur. There was the time, for example, when Flem got rid of Trumbull the old blacksmith, brought in Eck and I. O. Snopes to run the business, built a new shop and hired a new smith, sold the new shop including the smith to Will Varner, sold the old equipment to a junkman, moved the new equipment to the old shop, and finally sold the new building to a farmer who moved it away at his own expense. By this time Jody, Ratliff imagined, would be hysterically imploring Flem: " 'I want to make one pure and simple demand of you and I want a pure and simple Yes and No for a answer: How many more is there? How much longer is this going on? Just what is it going to cost me to protect one goddamn barn full of hay?' " (76)

When Ratliff learned, on his return from the Memphis hospital, of the arrival of still more Snopeses and of Flem's increasing activities (like making loans at usurous rates to country Negroes), he knew it was time to act. The two notes he had got from Mink Snopes on the purchase of a sewing machine afforded him both the chance of checking Flem and the pleasure of matching wits with him. So he baited a trap with goats and almost caught the rascal. But he failed to identify the name Ike Snopes with the shambling figure he had seen dragging a wooden block through the dust, the eyes "blasted empty and clean forever of any thought, the slobbering mouth in its mist of soft gold hair" (98); and he failed to reckon with his own sense of pity and shame. The realization that it was the idiot's money he and Flem were bargaining over filled him with a feeling of "suffocation, a sickness, a nausea" (97). He was deeply stirred by the pathos of the idiot's helplessness, by the look of uncomprehending suffering in its eyes as if it had been vouchsafed a glimpse of "the Gorgon-face of that primal injustice which man was not intended to look at face to face" (98), and by his own quizzical but conscience-stricken recognition that the idiot and he were "made in His image" (93). He could not use the idiot's note against Flem. The contest ended in a draw; whether he was smarter than Flem, Ratliff admitted, "aint been proved yet" (101).

Book Two turns from barter to love, from Flem Snopes to Eula Varner. These two characters—they are more symbol than person—represent two different principles of life: one the acquisitive, the other the sexual power. For Faulkner the latter is the more powerful and ambivalent force. The sexuality that the author incarnates in Eula Varner is both sacred and bestial. "Fecund and foul" (135), "unchaste and inviola- ble" (131), she is the "unawares bitch" (149) and the eternal goddess. In Swinburnian rhetoric he pays tribute to her as "some symbology out of the old Dionysic times—honey in sunlight and bursting grapes, the writhen bleeding of the crushed fecundated vine beneath the hard rapacious tram- pling goat-hoof" (107); but he derides her too in village style: " 'She's just like a dog! Soon as she passes anything in long pants she begins to give off something. You can smell it! You can smell it ten feet away!' " (112) However comic Eula's sexuality may be made to appear at times, it is a felt power. It embroils man in an endless struggle with woman and himself. The more puritan the society and the more in- tense the man, the more bitter the struggle. The power of woman enthralls and destroys. Its first victim was the school- teacher Labove.

Labove is a fantastic Faulknerian character. Faulkner de- scribes him as "a man who was not thin so much as actually

gaunt, with straight black hair coarse as a horse's tail and
high Indian cheekbones and quiet pale hard eyes and the
long nose of thought but with the slightly curved nostrils of
pride and the thin lips of secret and ruthless ambition" (119).
A dirt-farmer's son from the back hills, he was made gaunt
by the "consuming fury" (120-121) of his ambition and his
own nature. He had a "contemptuous intensity" (125) of
pride and dedication that one associates with a genius or
madman. This was the man who fell victim to an eleven-
year-old school girl. His passion was not love, it was terror
and hatred. He struggled against her, like a monk fighting
"his own fierce and unappeasable natural appetites" (119).
He was obsessed. "He did not want her as a wife, he just
wanted her one time as a man with a gangrened hand or
foot thirsts after the axe-stroke which will leave him com-
paratively whole again" (134). "Then one afternoon he found
his axe" (136): he assaulted her. As they wrestled and she
resisted, he said, " 'Fight it. Fight it. That's what it is: a man
and a woman fighting each other. The hating. To kill, only
to do it in such a way that the other will have to know forever afterward he or she is dead' " (138). Eula knocked him
to the floor. " 'Stop pawing me,' she said. 'You old headless
horseman Ichabod Crane' " (138).

Veering suddenly into comedy,[11] Faulkner breaks the intense obsessional tone of the Labove episode. Yet Labove's

---

11 After his assault upon Eula, Labove sought out Jody as if he desired violence from the brother's hand. At the moment he got ready
to open the door to the store, he remembered a scene at a railway
station: a white man ran cursing after a Negro and shot him in the
body. "Clutching his middle, his eyes closed and his face quite peaceful" (142), the Negro said as a doctor tried to break his hold: " 'Look
out, white folks, I awready been shot' " (142). But when they finally
unclasped his hands and peeled away jumper, overalls, coat, shirt and
trousers, "the bullet rolled out onto the platform, bloodless" (143).
On the same comic note ends Labove's encounter with Jody: prosaic
reality comically displaces the tragic mood.

obsession seems to mirror an outlook shared by the author—
even the comedy reflects its influence—and presents a major
thesis of the novel: that female sexuality is a power destructive of man and that sexual love is an act of aggression based
on hate and lust. Although the author may have shared some
of Labove's animus against woman and sex, he recognized
that it disqualified Labove as Eula's lover. Eula was waiting,
preserving her chastity "as if she really knew what instant,
moment, she was reserved for, even if not his name and face,
and was waiting for that moment" (146-147). The lover who
qualified was the bold sadistic young rake, Hoake McCarron; and the moment for which Eula had been preparing for
sixteen years of conspicuous ripening arrived after she and
he had fought off his rivals. The fight, the bloodshed, and the
broken arm of McCarron were the natural concomitants to
the defloration of Eula Varner. Her maidenhead broken, the
tone of the story changes and the comedy ensues. With Jody
as its instigator, the squabble over her impregnation raged
furiously in the house. While Jody fought with his father for
a pistol, Mrs. Varner, out of breath from running downstairs,
gasped forth: " 'Hold him till I get a stick of stove wood. . . .
I'll fix him. I'll fix both of them. Turning up pregnant and
yelling and cursing here in the house when I'm trying to take
a nap!' " (163) Then Will wrenched the pistol from his son
and dispatched him to the barn to cool his heels. It was the
old man who "cheerfully and robustly and undeviatingly de-
clined to accept any such theory as female chastity other
than as a myth to hoodwink young husbands" (160) that had
the last word on the rape of his daughter: " 'Hell and damna-
tion, all this hullabaloo and uproar because one confounded
running bitch finally foxed herself. What did you expect—
that she would spend the rest of her life just running water
through it?' " (164-165)

Book Three presents another variation on the theme of

love—an idiot's love for an animal. Paradoxically this story of rural sodomy is told in *The Hamlet*'s most elevated and lyric prose. So unabashedly poetic and richly allusive is the language that one might suspect a parody, except that the author seems genuinely moved by certain qualities in the romance of Ike and his cow. It is not so much a story as a lyric fantasia, a poem that springs out of an elemental love and a poetic joy in nature. The idiot, T. Y. Greet has remarked, is like a lover in a medieval romance who rescues his love from fire and dragon.[12] But it is the devotion rather than the heroism that makes Ike Snopes the truest lover in the novel. For Labove and McCarron love was lust, for Flem a commodity to be bartered.[13] Only in an idiot's passion has Faulkner found an unbrutalized and uncorrupted love, as if the idiot represented a state of nature. The pinehills where Ike and the cow took refuge from the world suggest, too, nature unravished by man.[14] The "shaggy crests" of the pines made "a constant murmuring sound in the high serene air," as if the trunks and massy foliage were the "harps and strings of afternoon" (205). For the few days they lived in their Eden, the sun was their guide. Dawn came like a slow burst

---

[12] See T. Y. Greet, "The Theme and Structure of Faulkner's *The Hamlet*," in *William Faulkner: Three Decades of Criticism*, p.340.

[13] Flem's idea of love is revealed not only in his successful trade of Mrs. Eula Snopes for money and the Old Frenchman place, but in an imaginary scene (Ratliff is the imaginer) that depicts Flem fornicating with a Negress fieldhand upon the floor of Varner's store, the payment to be a nickel's worth of lard (187-188).

[14] That the idiot's Eden is part of a fantasy is pointed up in an earlier passage that described the inroads of the sawmills upon the pinehills, "their sites marked only by the mounds of rotting sawdust which were not only their gravestones but the monuments of a people's heedless greed. Now it was a region of scrubby second-growth pine and oak . . . and old fields where not even a trace of furrow showed any more, gutted and gullied by forty years of rain and frost and heat into plateaus choked with rank sedge and briers" (196).

of "jonquil thunder" (207), and the lovers advanced with the rising sun.

They have the same destination: sunset. They pursue it as the sun itself does and within the compass of one single immutable horizon. They pace the ardent and unheeding sun, themselves unheeding and without ardor among the shadows of the soaring trunks which are the sun-geared ratchet-spokes which wheel the axled earth, powerful and without haste, up out of the caverns of darkness, through dawn and morning and midmorning, and on toward and at last into the slowing neap of noon, the flood, the slack of peak and crown of light garlanding all within one single coronet the fallen and unregenerate seraphim. (210)

Even a sudden lancing shower of rain did not put out Ike's joy.[15] Still the lovers "walk in splendor. Joined by the golden skein of the wet grass rope, they move in single file toward the ineffable effulgence, directly into the sun" (212). At nightfall as the earth wheeled darkly under the evening star,

she is there, solid amid the abstract earth. He walks lightly upon it, returning, treading lightly that frail inextricable canopy of the subterrene slumber—Helen and the bishops, the kings and the graceless seraphim. When he reaches her, she has already begun to lie down—first the forequarters, then the hinder ones, lowering herself in two distinct stages into the spent ebb of evening, nestling back into the nest-form of sleep, the mammalian attar. They lie down together. (213)

The Keatsian poetry of the language evokes another world where reality has been suspended and the poet's imagination rules: the idiot and the cow might be lovers out of a storied

---

[15] Peter Lisca has commented interestingly on the significance of the setting and the shower: "Their [the lovers'] 'honeymoon' is idyllic in a poetic landscape, their very union sanctioned, like that of Dido and Aeneas, by symbolic lightning (the heavens fertilizing the earth), thunder and a shower of rain, the idiot, loverlike, bringing delicacies and garlands of wild flowers to his loved one." See Lisca, loc. cit., p.12.

past who, at one with nature and themselves, partake of a
serene ineffable moment when time no longer exists.

But the idiot's idyll was a fragile doomed dream the world
would shatter. The old farmer from whom Ike stole feed,
Houston from whom he stole the cow, and Ratliff whose
morality he affronted represent the property rights and puritanism of Frenchman's Bend that separate Ike from his cow.[16]
The debasement of Ike's passion into a sideshow for the titil-
lation of the village males makes Ratliff's opposition necessary and prepares us to accept the defeat of Mrs. Littlejohn's
compassion for the idiot by Ratliff's morality. Although Ratliff's sense of decency prevails over the pathos of the idiot's
loss, Faulkner suggests that the idiot is in one sense superior
to the community. The idiot's passion remains pure; but for
the others, just as "Lancelot" would degenerate into "Lump,"
so would love degenerate into lust, and the idiot's "wordless
passions" into the village's "specious words" (224). A nostalgic sense of loss in Faulkner reaches back to the innocent
stage of life when man had not yet acquired "lust and greed
and bloodthirst and a moral conscience to keep him awake
at night" (209).

Still it is the "lust and greed and bloodthirst and a moral
conscience" that provide the novel with its dramatic material,
particularly in the next episode. A story of murder and retribution, the Houston-Mink Snopes episode is concerned nevertheless with the theme of love or rather with the struggle
between the sexes which is part of love. The feud between
the female passion for the married state and the masculine
need for freedom dominated the youth of Jack Houston.
Even as a boy Houston sensed that underlying Lucy Pate's
"constancy and devotion" (235) and "proffered slavedom"

---

16 Although Houston eventually gives up the cow to Ike, in most of
the story he separates the idiot from the "damned whore" (191, 200).

(237) was that "unflagging will . . . for the married state" (238), "that single constant despotic undeviating will of the enslaved not only for possession, complete assimilation, but to coerce and reshape the enslaver into the seemliness of his victimization" (237). To escape the "immemorial trap" (235) he fled to the West, from Lucy Pate to a Galveston whore as if he could escape "from one woman by violating the skirts of another" (242). He stayed away for thirteen years. But Lucy Pate was the love and trap he could not escape. "Bitted now" (245) and "drawn to the trap" (246), he came back to marry her. He built her a house and bought her new furniture and appliances. When the women remarked "how the house had been completed exactly in time to catch the moon's full of April through the window where the bed was placed" (247), her plain face bloomed "with something almost like beauty" (246). April however was when the stallion—in a sense it was his wedding gift to her, for it signified "that polygamous and bitless masculinity which he had relinquished" (246)—killed her. He gave up everything except his grief, and he grieved for her "in black, savage, indomitable fidelity" (235). The bad times were the April nights when the moon was full:

there was no body beside his own for the moon to fall upon, and nothing for another body to have lain beside his own upon. Because the cot was too narrow for that and there was only the abrupt downward sheer of inky shadow in which only the invisible hound slept, and he would lie rigid, indomitable, and panting. "I dont understand it," he would say. "I dont know why. I wont ever know why. But You cant beat me. I am strong as You are. You cant beat me." (248-249)

Then Mink Snopes shot him.

Murderer and victim are in many respects strangely alike. Proud and tough, both had run away from home in their

youth: one to flee the trap of marriage, the other to repudiate
the sharecropping existence into which he had been born.
Neither had found freedom, and both had returned to the
land and married state which seemed their fate. But Mink,
smaller in size and less successful in farming, was doomed to
a frustration that drove him to desperate resistance and vindication. Fate had made him small; hence he married a nymphomaniac as if he had to compete "with men among whom
he saw himself . . . as a child" who "would have to tear aside
not garments alone but the ghostly embraces of thirty or forty
men" (272). However, he could never efface the image of his
wife "as she was standing in the savage lamplight, above the
loud harsh voices of invisible men, in the open door of the
mess-hall in that south Mississippi convict camp where he
first saw her nine years ago" (252). It was the same image
he saw on the night she prepared to leave him (254), the
same image he saw on the night she came running out of
the Varner doorway with the money she had earned by ped-
dling her body (269-271). Fate had compounded humiliation
with humiliation. It had fixed him too in a sorry rented cabin
"just like the one he had been born in which had not belonged
to his father either, and just like the one he would die in"
and "just like the more than six others he had lived in since
his marriage and like the twice that many more he knew he
would live in before he did die" (251). For Mink fate and
the world were conspiring "to frustrate and outrage his rights
as a man and his feelings as a sentient creature" (251). So
he pulled the trigger not only against the man who had im-
pounded his yearling but against the whole scheme of his
existence. And he found that as with his marriage he had not
just vindicated his manhood, he had taken on another burden.

There were a corpse to bury and a hound to silence. For
four weary days and nights, in which he was borne only by

the "singleness of his will" (260), he applied himself to the task. But he could not put the corpse away. When he tried to hide it in the big hollow oak stump, it jammed on him, and he had to jump up and down on it until corpse and murderer fell together to the bottom. For a terrible while as the edge of the rotten shell of the high stump crumbled beneath his clutching fingers, "he climbed interminably, furiously perpetual and without gain, his mouth open for his panting breath and his eyes glaring at the remote September sky" (259). The scene, with its harrowing sense of entrapment, seems a nightmare epiphany of Mink Snopes's life. Murder was his last protest against the entrapment. Yet just as he was wedded forever to the "cuckolding shades" (254) of his wife's lovers, so was he "wedded and twinned forever now by the explosion of that ten-gauge shell" (249) to the man he had murdered. The hound's griefstricken cries pursued him like the furies of old, but he would not admit to pangs of conscience. For Mink the hound was but a hound, the corpse a corpse. It was his will against conscience; it was an unadmitted struggle between the pride which isolated him and the conscience which bound him to society. To the very end he insisted it was not the hound that beat him but the body's coming to pieces. " 'Hush, white man,' the negro [in the jail] said. 'Hush. Dont be telling us no truck like that' " (296).

The story of Mink is part of the novel's "intricate patterning of contrasts":[17] Mink's love is set in contrast with the idiot's (with the others' too but less explicitly), and toward the end of the story Mink himself is set in contrast with his cousin Lump. The mood of the idiot's romance is pastoral and lyrical, its setting the pinehills in May; the mood of the

---

[17] Robert Penn Warren, "The Snopes World," *Kenyon Review*, 3 (Spring 1941), 256.

murderer's story is sullen and nightmarish, its setting the swamp in dry September. As the idiot fled from the world, he was paced by the sun and walked in splendor; as Mink tried to thwart law and conscience, he ran alone and lost through the dark bottom. Ike was ruled by innocence and tenderness, Mink by pride and grievance. The idiot's idyll was only a fantasy; Mink's story was the actuality. Part of life's actuality in Frenchman's Bend was the concern for money. As Lump's irrepressible greed for the money on the corpse persists in the face of Mink's unconcern and desperate weariness, comedy mixes with pathos in a strangely effective counterpoint. The effect is to isolate Mink still further and to enhance his lonely resistant pride. In his own misdirected way Mink was indomitable.

Book Four comes back to the subject and mood of Book One, turning from the somber dramas of individuals to the folk comedy of the community, from intense oppressive feelings to the relaxed humorous atmosphere of the gatherings of men on the galleries of Varner's Store or Littlejohn's Hotel or by the fence of Mrs. Littlejohn's lot. The arrival of the spotted horses provides a circus excitement for the hamlet as well as another chance to buy something from Flem Snopes. Although Ratliff heads the opposition to Flem, since he is most disturbed by the Snopes threat, he serves in his role of ironic commentator to reinforce the comic mood. In the spotted horse episode comedy rules. There are the wry sarcasm and understatement of the farmers' remarks, the shrewd irony of the exchanges between Varner and Ratliff, and the exaggerated contrast between the Texan's spiel on the ponies' gentleness and his incredibly violent struggles with them described in superb poetic hyperboles:

"Look him over, boys," the Texan panted, turning his own suffused face and the protuberant glare of his eyes toward the fence. "Look him over quick. Them shoulders and—" He had relaxed for an instant apparently. The animal exploded again; again for an instant the Texan was free of the earth, though he was still talking: "—and legs you whoa I'll tear your face right look him over quick boys worth fifteen dollars of let me get a holt of who'll make me a bid whoa you blare-eyed jack rabbit, whoa!" They were moving now—a kaleidoscope of inextricable and incredible violence on the periphery of which the metal clasps of the Texan's suspenders sun-glinted in ceaseless orbit, with terrific slowness across the lot. Then the broad clay-colored hat soared deliberately outward; an instant later the Texan followed it, though still on his feet, and the pony shot free in mad, staglike bounds. (329)

It was a foregone conclusion that the farmers, despite Ratliff's advice and their own awareness of their "puerile folly,"[18] would buy the spotted horses. The horses seem to represent an untamed masculine violence or freedom (associated with the "bitless masculinity" of Houston's stallion) that appealed to the farmers by its exciting difference from the simple routine of their lives. Violence, latent and explosive, dominates the auction scene. The scene has the qualities of both a painting and a motion picture: in the foreground the horses rushed with purposeless fury back and forth across the lot while the Texan harangued the idle men; in the background Mrs. Littlejohn went about her chores, commenting by her work and presence on all masculine tomfoolery. Ratliff (and the mockingbird) mocked the farmer's gullibility, but Mrs. Littlejohn, Mrs. Tull, and Mrs. Armstid condemned the whole masculine race: Mrs. Littlejohn by her practicality and sardonic remarks, Mrs. Tull by her angry tirades in court, and Mrs. Armstid by her suffering at the hands of her mad hus-

---

[18] This phrase is part of Faulkner's answer to a question on the symbolism of the horses: "they symbolized the hope, the aspiration of the masculine part of society that is capable of doing, of committing puerile folly for some gewgaw that has drawn him, as juxtaposed to the cold practicality of the women whose spokesman Mrs. Littlejohn was when she said 'Them men'" (*Faulkner in the University*, p.66).

band. Despite the pathos of Mrs. Armstid's plight, the war
between the sexes remains comic. The fury of the horses, as
they explode from Mrs. Littlejohn's lot over the countryside,
sweeps away all concerns and makes for a general hilarity.
Eck's horse—whirling through Mrs. Littlejohn's hall "like a
pinwheel, gaudy, furious and thunderous" (345), scaring
Ratliff into a dive through the open window, running smack
into Mrs. Littlejohn's washboard and her " 'Get out of here,
you son of a bitch' " (346), soaring over the prone Eck and
the erect boy, galloping on up the road into Tull's sleepy
wagon and wreaking havoc among the Tull females and the
hapless male—Eck's horse sets the tone. Against the tremulous
beauty of the April moonlit night the men and the horses ran
madly about the countryside. All that remained was for Will
Varner to doctor the injured, Ratliff to make his final remarks,
and for the court suits against Snopes to end in the comic
explosions of Mrs. Tull.

The last episode, as one might expect, suffers a letdown
in its comic energy; it suffers a letdown too in its imaginative
power. The final battle of wits between the two principals,
Flem and Ratliff, has failed for some reason to engage the
full resources of the author. In adapting the original version
of the treasure hunt to *The Hamlet*, Faulkner has not changed
Suratt into the Ratliff who was the compassionate spokesman
for decency and humanity in Frenchman's Bend. The Ratliff
of this episode is too much like the mad Armstid, too much in
his money-lust like Flem himself. The blurring of the moral
difference between Flem and Ratliff, the abandonment of the
moral conflict between them has been justifiably regarded as
a weakness in the novel.[19] The whole episode reveals a lessening of the author's concern with the novel's moral issues;
a displacement of moral concern by the comic mood, as if the

---

[19] See, for example, Howe, op. cit., pp.183-184.

duel between Flem and Ratliff were only another variation
on the comic theme of barter; and lastly a realistic recognition that victory would go to the shrewder horsetrader. Because of its moral indifference the final episode seems inade-
quate, however, as a conclusion to a brilliant, tragicomic
novel, although from the point of view of form, the ending
is apt. The novel begins with the entrance of Flem into
Frenchman's Bend as a poor sharecropper and ends with his
departure as the successful trader looking for new fields to
conquer. At the end, as in *The Sound and the Fury*, the reins
remain in the hands of the man who, feeling no love and abiding by no morality, has reduced life to a horsetrade.

Flem Snopes and Jason Compson, though springing from
different milieus, are alike in that they are the comic antagonists who represent the overriding materialism of the world;
and the idiots in both novels are alike in that they are the
victims whose hunger for love will be thwarted by the world.
Both *The Sound and the Fury* and *The Hamlet* deal with the
loss of a sister's honor, which leads in the earlier work to a
brother's suicide and in the later to his comic dismissal.
Unlike Caddy, who was a tragic victim of her own desires
and her brother's love, Eula Varner is a comic-mythic symbol of the power of female sexuality; and her victim Labove
finds an answer to his struggle with his sexual instincts by
taking a bloodless departure from Varner territory. The tensions that underlie the comedy of *The Hamlet* are related to
those of *The Sound and the Fury*, but the novels are as different as the characters of Ratliff and Quentin Compson.
It is Ratliff's ironic, humorous perspective that dominates
The Hamlet, making comic that which was tragic eleven
years before; and his feeling for the people of Frenchman's
Bend marks the distance the Faulkner protagonist has trav-
eled from a suicidal isolation to a benign joining up with the
human race.

IO

"The Bear"
and *Go Down, Moses*

The heart of *Go Down, Moses* (1942) is "The Bear."
The most widely acclaimed story of the seven in the volume,
"The Bear" has received a variety of interpretations. One
critic has emphasized its New Testament spirit, others its
romantic and transcendental character, and still others its
primitivism and myth.[1] The variety of critical response testi-

---

[1] See R. W. B. Lewis, "The Hero in the New World: William Faulkner's 'The Bear'," in *Bear, Man, and God: Seven Approaches to William Faulkner's "The Bear,"* ed. Francis Lee Utley, Lynn Z. Bloom, and
Arthur F. Kinney (New York, Random House, 1964), pp.306-323;
Lionel Trilling, "The McCaslins of Mississippi," *The Nation,* 154 (May
30, 1942), 632-633; Irving D. Blum, "The Parallel Philosophy of Emerson's 'Nature' and Faulkner's 'The Bear'," *Emerson Society Quarterly,* No. 13 (4th Quarter, 1958), 22-25; Malcolm Cowley, "Go Down
to Faulkner's Land," *The New Republic,* 106 (June 29, 1942), 900;
Harry Modean Campbell and Ruel E. Foster, *William Faulkner: A
Critical Appraisal* (Norman, University of Oklahoma, 1951), pp.146-
158; Kenneth LaBudde, "Cultural Primitivism in William Faulkner's
'The Bear'," *American Quarterly,* 2 (Winter 1950), 322-328; William
Van O'Connor, "The Wilderness Theme in Faulkner's 'The Bear',"
Accent, 13 (Winter 1953), 12-20; W. R. Moses, "Where History
Crosses Myth: Another Reading of 'The Bear'," *Accent,* 13 (Winter
1953), 21-33; Otis B. Wheeler, "Faulkner's Wilderness," *American
Literature,* 31 (May 1959), 127-136; Herbert A. Perluck, " 'The
Heart's Driving Complexity': An Unromantic Reading of Faulkner's
'The Bear'," *Accent,* 20 (Winter 1960), 23-46; Stanley Sultan, "Call
Me Ishmael: The Hagiography of Isaac McCaslin," *Texas Studies in*

fies to the story's density of meaning. It is a rich, original story treating of a universal issue; nevertheless, it is distinctly American. Lionel Trilling has placed it in the romantic, transcendental tradition of Cooper, Thoreau, and Melville, while Malcolm Cowley has associated it with the work of Mark Twain. In its pastoral spirit "The Bear" does seem related to *Huck Finn;* and, in its development of the wilderness theme, to Cooper's *Leatherstocking Tales.*[2] Yet because of the story's tendency to split into two parts—one part concerned with the wilderness, the other with the Negro—the structure of the story has seemed faulty and its meaning ambiguous. If "The Bear" is examined within the context of the other related stories of the *Go Down, Moses* volume, its meaning may be clarified.

The first story, "Was," is a warmly humorous introduction to some of the old McCaslins, white and black, before the Civil War. The next two stories, "The Fire and the Hearth" and "Pantaloon in Black," turn their focus upon the Negro. But the following three stories—"The Old People," "The Bear," and "Delta Autumn"—shift to Isaac McCaslin and the wilderness. The last story, "Go Down, Moses," returns to the Negro. The movement of the *Go Down, Moses* volume is from surface to depth, from comedy to tragedy, and from the antebellum past to the present—about the beginning of the

---

Literature and Language, 3 (Spring 1961), 50-66; and Neal Woodruff, Jr., " 'The Bear' and Faulkner's Moral Vision," *Studies in Faulkner* (Pittsburgh, Pa., Carnegie Institute of Technology, 1961), 43-67. See also *Bear, Man, and God: Seven Approaches to William Faulkner's "The Bear,"* a collection of critical essays and background materials on "The Bear."

[2] Ursula Brumm has commented on the relationship between Cooper and Faulkner, particularly in regard to the wilderness theme and the affinity between Sam Fathers and Natty Bumppo. See Ursula Brumm, "Wilderness and Civilization: A Note on William Faulkner," *Partisan Review,* 22 (Summer 1955), 340-350.

Second World War. The subject of *Go Down, Moses* is apparently the Negro or the wilderness, although in "The Bear"
they are strangely merged. This merging of the Negro and
the wilderness suggests that "The Bear" is not only the heart
but also the climax of *Go Down, Moses,* since this collection
of stories about the black and white descendants of the Mc-
Caslin clan of the last century is concerned, in a sense, with
the making of the conscience of Isaac McCaslin. It seems appropriate, therefore, to begin this study of "The Bear" with
a discussion of the Negro, particularly as he emerges in "The
Fire and the Hearth," and later, after a close consideration of
"The Bear" itself, to conclude with Faulkner's final commentary on the wilderness and the Negro in "Delta Autumn" and
"Go Down, Moses."

"The Fire and the Hearth" is concerned with two themes:
(1) the Negro-white relationship and (2) family love. Its
hero is the Negro, Lucas Beauchamp. Lucas was a proud
Negro who had fought for his rights as a man. There was the
time he went to fetch his wife from the white man's house
where she had gone six months ago to deliver and nurse the
white child, Roth Edmonds. Lucas confronted Zack Edmonds, his white kinsman and landlord: " 'I'm a nigger. . . .
But I'm a man too. I'm more than just a man. The same thing
made my pappy that made your grandmaw. I'm going to
take her back' " (47).[3] She came back. But six months of
jealous brooding had driven a hot iron into Lucas' pride.
The next night he went to the white man's house to kill his
kinsman. They had once lived as brothers: "they had fished
and hunted together, they had learned to swim in the same
water, they had eaten at the same table in the white boy's
kitchen and in the cabin of the negro's mother; they had slept

---

[3] *Go Down, Moses* (New York, Modern Library, 1955); page references are to this edition.

under the same blanket before a fire in the woods" (55). But that was long ago. Now Lucas was protesting against the white man's prerogative over the black man's wife. That he was wrong in his suspicions is beside the point. He had to protest in order to assert the manhood that Southern heritage denied the Negro.

The fire in the hearth which Lucas had lit on his wedding day in 1895 "was to burn on the hearth until neither he nor Molly were left to feed it" (47). This fire is symbolic of love. It is not the kind of love that Faulkner treated in *The Wild Palms* or *The Hamlet;* it is more akin to the warm affection that bound the MacCallum family together in *Sartoris.* In *Sartoris* that love was associated with life; its absence, as illustrated in Bayard's self-destructive course, with death. In "The Fire and the Hearth" love is threatened and invaded by the inherited curse which separates white from black.

The "old curse" (111) descended too upon the next generation—on Roth, the son of Zack, and Henry, the son of Lucas. For seven years the boys had played together, eaten together and slept together—the white boy even preferring the Negro cabin with its ever-burning fire—until one night the white boy had insisted that Henry sleep separately in the pallet below the bed. That night the white boy lay "in a rigid fury of the grief he could not explain, the shame he would not admit" (112). They never slept again in the same room nor ate at the same table. The price for white supremacy was shame and loss of love.

Both as boy and man, Roth Edmonds is characterized as deprived of love. The only mother he had ever known was the little Negress, Molly. It was she

who had raised him, fed him from her own breast as she was actually doing her own child, who had surrounded him always with care for his physical body and for his spirit too, teaching

him his manners, behavior—to be gentle with his inferiors, honorable with his equals, generous to the weak and considerate of the
aged, courteous, truthful and brave to all—who had given him,
the motherless, without stint or expectation of reward that constant and abiding devotion and love which existed nowhere else
in this world for him. (117)

He had lived his early life in the Negro cabin where "a little
fire always burned, centering the life in it, to his own" (110).
Living as brother to Henry, he had wanted "only to love . . .
and to be let alone" (111). But that was his lost childhood
which he had to forsake for the prerogatives of his Southern
heritage. Southern heritage denied the black brother Roth's
love and denied the white boy his brother's and mother's
love. Faulkner's concern over this deprivation of love is not
new, for the "tragic complexity . . . of motherless childhood"
(130-131) echoes through Faulkner's novels. Many of his
isolated and defeated protagonists—Quentin Compson, Joe
Christmas, Joanna Burden, Gail Hightower, and Charles Bon
—are marked by a motherless childhood. Behind the malaise
and violence in Faulkner's works is the lost affection of childhood. But in *Go Down, Moses* the love that has been destroyed is the brotherhood between white and black.

The nostalgia for a lost love and innocence is central to
"The Bear" too, although it has been enriched and transfigured in this story of the wilderness, since Faulkner has
made use of a theme—a point of view, in fact—deeply embedded in American literature. In the conscious and unconscious memory of the American writer, the woods and rivers
have loomed large because of their associations with a primitive and natural existence, free from the restraints and corruption of civilization. For Cooper the wilderness retained a
primeval beauty and calm, though the simple, heroic Indians
and Natty Bumppo had to yield to the destructive and pos-
sessive settlers. Based in part on the American frontier expe-

rience, the nostalgia for a primitive past seems to derive chiefly, however, from the author's own needs. This nostalgia often turns back to childhood—as if searching consciously for a lost innocence and freedom, and unconsciously for a lost peace. It is clearly evident in *Tom Sawyer* and *Huck Finn*. In *Tom Sawyer* the golden age of life is the carefree, joyous summertime of boyhood. In *Huck Finn* a boy and a slave, rafting down the friendly Mississippi, establish a brief idyll of peace and natural fellowship; but from the land come the representatives of civilization, armed with greed and deceit and violence, to shatter the idyll. The same opposition between nature and civilization, the same desire to retreat to an earlier, more natural way of life is apparent in "The Bear."

For the orphan Isaac McCaslin his true home would become the wilderness; his true father an old Indian who, quitting the plantation, returned to the wilderness whence he had derived. There as a self-appointed guardian of the woods Sam Fathers was to live out his remaining years. But already —it was 1877—the woods were "that doomed wilderness whose edges were being constantly and punily gnawed at by men with plows and axes who feared it because it was wilderness" (193). In the face of its inevitable destruction, the old Indian trained the boy for initiation into the wilderness as though he were its priest and the boy the novitiate. But if Sam Fathers was the priest of the wilderness, Old Ben was its chief. To pass the ordeal of initiation the boy would have to win acceptance from the chief. To accomplish this the boy had to shed the instruments and symbols of civilization: the gun, watch, and compass. He had to conquer his fear, discipline his will, and, finally, like a humble suppliant before his god, surrender himself completely to the wilderness. The boy's communion was confirmed by the silent, mystical appearance of Old Ben.

Not long after the boy's initiation Sam Fathers found the

dog who was brave enough, worthy enough to hunt the old
bear. The dog possessed the hunter's fierce implacability—
"the will and desire to pursue and kill . . . to endure beyond
all imaginable limits of flesh in order to overtake and slay"
(237)—that had been "ordered and compelled by and within
the wilderness" (191-192). This was the dog—they had
named him Lion—who would be pitted against the bear in
the last great hunt. These two kings of beasts seemed the
sole surviving representatives of the ancient life and hunt
of the wilderness. In the hunt that brooked no quarter, death
was inevitable. The boy knew it, yet he did not hate Lion.
"It seemed to him that there was a fatality in it. It seemed
to him that something, he didn't know what, was beginning;
had already begun. It was like the last act on a set stage.
It was the beginning of the end of something" (226). Despite these apprehensions he did not fully realize that the
death of Old Ben signified the impending death of the wilderness. But Sam knew it. When Old Ben went down, "as a
tree falls" (241), "the old man, the wild man not even one
generation from the woods, childless, kinless, peopleless,"
(246) prepared to die too.

Joining Lion's attack upon the bear was the half-breed
Indian, Boon Hogganbeck, who followed the dog as if Lion
were his totem and represented his almost forsaken Indian
heritage. Boon's killing of Old Ben entitles him to glory,
but it has involved him too in the white man's guilt in the
destruction of the woods. Boon served Major de Spain and
McCaslin Edmonds. It was men like these who were destroying the wilderness—the Major by selling the woods to the
lumber interests, McCaslin by clearing its borders in order
to build farms and fill his bank's coffers. Great hunter for
the moment, Boon was also an unwitting instrument of the
wilderness' destruction. Of this the boy was dimly aware;

hence he stood apart from the action of the hunt, as if his will to act were paralyzed by his conflicting identification with both the hunted and the hunter. The ambivalence of the boy is embedded in the story itself, so that though "The Bear" celebrates the glory of the hunt, it mourns elegiacally the passing of the wilderness.

Implicit in the story is the dream of the wilderness as idyllic retreat, as an escape from the outside world to a reassuring but solitary peace. Like the river in *Huck Finn*, the woods in "The Bear" represents a retreat for a boy and a man, and like the river's idyll it was doomed to extinction by civilization. For Issac McCaslin the woods came, more and more, to signify escape from woman, from the world and struggle. The figures to whom he surrendered, Old Ben and Sam Fathers, were solitary old bachelors identified with the wilderness. It was the wilderness that he embraced, the land that he repudiated. He had to repudiate, he explained to his cousin McCaslin Edmonds, because the land that did not belong to his father or grandfather or even Ikkemotubbe could not be bequeathed to him.

Because He told in the Book how He created the earth, made it and looked at it and said it was all right, and then He made man. He made the earth first and peopled it with dumb creatures, and then He created man to be His overseer on the earth and to hold suzerainty over the earth and the animals on it in His name, not to hold for himself and his descendants inviolable title forever, generation after generation, to the oblongs and squares of the earth, but to hold the earth mutual and intact in the communal anonymity of brotherhood. . . . (257)

For Isaac the golden age was the wilderness time when men lived as brothers before they had become tainted by the greed for possession. This primitivistic communism is not a new idea in Faulkner's works. In "Lo" (1935) an Indian reminded the President that "God's forest and the deer which He put in it belong to all"; in Thomas Sutpen's mountain home "the land belonged to anybody and everybody"; in "Retreat" (1938) Buck and Buddy McCaslin believed that "land did not belong to people but that people belonged to land." But it remained for Isaac McCaslin to develop this idea into a philosophy for life.[4] This philosophy ran absolutely counter to that of his ancestor, Old Carothers. Carothers "took the land, got the land no matter how, held it to bequeath, no matter how, out of the old grant, the first patent, when it was a wilderness of wild beasts and wilder men, and cleared it, translated it into something to bequeath to his children, worthy of bequeathment for his descendants' ease and security and pride and to perpetuate his name and accomplishments" (256). All that Old Carothers represented Isaac was repudiating.

However, that he repudiated out of his belief in God's communistic scheme seems a rationalization of a more deeply rooted motive. He was driven to repudiation by the guilt inherited from the McCaslin sin against the Negro, a sin which had long since tainted the land. He first became aware

---

[4] Despite the relationship of this philosophy to the Indian and frontier point of view, the philosophy may stem from Rousseau's "Discourse on Inequality." Rousseau wrote: "The first man, who, after enclosing a piece of ground, took it into his head to say, 'This is mine,' and found people simple enough to believe him, was the true founder of civil society. How many crimes, how many wars, how many murders, how many misfortunes and horrors, would that man have saved the human species, who pulling up the stakes or filling up the ditches should have cried to his fellows: Be sure not to listen to this imposter; you are lost, if you forget that the fruits of the earth belong equally to us all, and the earth itself to nobody!" Compare Faulkner's remark in *Absalom, Absalom!* (Modern Library, p.221): "Where he [the boy Thomas Sutpen] lived the land belonged to anybody and everybody and so the man who would go to the trouble and work to fence off a piece of it and say 'This is mine' was crazy."

of this sin when he was a boy of sixteen. In the "rank chill midnight room" (271) of the McCaslin commissary he pored over the entries on the yellowed pages of the old ledgers. He was learning about his black kin: Eunice, who drowned herself in the creek on Christmas Day, 1832; Tomey, her daughter, who died in childbirth six months later; and the son Terrel, who was born in Tomey's death. Tomey's Terrel had been marked down in Old Carothers' will for a thousand dollar legacy. Yes, Isaac thought, his grandfather had found it cheaper to give a thousand dollars than to say "My son to a nigger" (269). And Isaac thought of the young girl, Tomey: had there been any love between the old man and her, or had it been "just an afternoon's or a night's spitoon" (270)? Suddenly he realized the truth: his grandfather had taken not only his slave but also "his own daughter" (270). He knew now why Eunice had drowned herself. He saw that the McCaslin chronicle "was a whole land in miniature, which multiplied and compounded was the entire South" (293), the "whole edifice . . . founded upon injustice and erected by ruthless rapacity and carried on even yet with at times downright savagery" (298). The Southern planters "were all Grandfather" (283). They had denied the heart's rights to their black kin; they had sold themselves to rapacity. Where were the "humility and pity and sufferance and pride of one to another" (258) upon which God had founded and granted the new world to man? These virtues were part of the dream to which Isaac clung desperately in the face of his knowledge of the South's miscegenation and incest.

In Faulkner's novels incest tragically complicates the lives of his heroes and forces them to decisions that determine the course of their own and their descendants' lives. Quentin Compson yielded to the incestuous attraction of his sister Caddy; the result was his death by suicide. Charles Bon

decided to marry his white sister; the result was his death
by murder. Bayard Sartoris ("An Odor of Verbena") resisted
his stepmother's offer of herself; the result was life and increased moral strength. Old Carothers took his slave-daughter
Tomey; the result was the sin that oppressed his descendants'
conscience. Incest and miscegenation have been deeply
rooted in the Southern past; they have evolved from the
white planter's freedom with his women slaves and have
produced his double family—black and white. The white
planter and his offspring were enmeshed in tragic conflicts
and contradictions. On one hand, the South, with its emphasis
upon family and honor, promoted strong familial bonds and
obligations; on the other hand, the South refused to accord
family status and love to a white man's black offspring. The
black man's life was tragically scarred; the white man's conscience was grievously burdened.

To make a life of their own the black grandchildren of Old
Carothers abandoned the plantation in the 1880's. Tennie's
Jim vanished forever somewhere in Tennessee in December
1885; seven months later Fonsiba went off with an educated
Negro; only Lucas stayed on the plantation. To fulfill his
grandfather's will and to ease his own conscience, Isaac went
in search of Fonsiba. He found her living with her scholar-
husband in Midnight, Arkansas. They were living with their
delusion of freedom in a cold and empty cabin on an un-
fenced piece of jungle land. For Isaac these Negroes who had
abandoned the plantation to embrace freedom and education
were dwelling in darkness and delusion, as well as misery and
poverty. It was twenty-two years after the Emancipation
Proclamation, and still they were not free.

. Neither was Isaac free, even after his repudiation of the
cursed land in 1889. He had to repudiate, he told his cousin
McCaslin, " 'because I have got myself to have to live with

for the rest of my life and all I want is peace to do it in' " (288).
But there was no peace. At the same time that Isaac was
seeking to atone for the inherited sin, he was paralyzingly
aware of the futility of his repudiation. Underlying his noble
words is a sense of desperation and grieving helplessness.
He cried out to Fonsiba's husband:

'Dont you see? This whole land, the whole South, is cursed, and
all of us who derive from it, whom it ever suckled, white and
black both, lie under the curse? Granted that my people brought
the curse onto the land: maybe for that reason their descendants
alone can—not resist it, not combat it—maybe just endure and out-
last it until the curse is lifted. Then your peoples' turn will come
because we have forfeited ours. But not now. Not yet. Dont you
see?' (278)

To the question of how long the land would be cursed, Isaac
replied to McCaslin: " 'It will be long.... But it will be all
right because they [the Negroes] will endure' " (299). Isaac
has offered the Negro the consolation that the Negro will
endure, and the blind faith that the wrong will be righted
if one does nothing long enough.

Yet this defeatism is not the complete measure of Isaac
McCaslin; it is but the partial response of an embattled and
struggling spirit. Isaac, like the story itself, is torn in two
by opposing forces. One force moves him to atone for the
sin against the Negro; the other pushes him toward escape
from the Southern dilemma. To atone for the sin, he repudiated the land; but this proved to be only a lonely gesture of
the conscience that did not touch the hard face of the world.
To escape the dilemma he sought refuge in the wilderness,
where "he would be able to hide himself" (318). Like its
protagonist, "The Bear" both retreats from and confronts
life. When it retreats from the Southern situation, it tells
beautifully and mystically of the hunt and the wilderness,

as though chanting an elegy for the passing of a golden age.
When the story confronts the Southern dilemma, it loses
focus and disintegrates. This is most apparent in the fourth
section of the story, which rambles from Isaac's discursive
introversions to the ledger entries, to various uncorrelated
episodes, and finally to the intrusive opinions of the author
about the relative merits of the South and the North. Both
the protagonist and the author seem to be battling with
themselves—not in the manner of the author of *Absalom,
Absalom!* or *The Sound and the Fury* with its fine controlled
tension, but in the manner of one who is being fragmented
by unbearable guilt. It is not just the South's obsessional guilt
about the Negro, it is the guilt implicit in a public admission
of sin—a treasonable act for a Southerner.

By shifting the story's focus from the Negro to the wilderness, Faulkner is shifting the burden of guilt from the South
to mankind. It is mankind that, driven by rapacity, has destroyed God's wilderness and enslaved His black creatures.
Although the exploitation of nature is not morally the same
as the enslavement of one's fellow man, Faulkner has chosen
to merge these two crimes, as if to blur their moral distinc-
tions. By fashioning a primitivistic mystique, with Christian
overtones, based on God's will and the concept of the virgin
wilderness as the golden age, Faulkner has endeavored to
bulwark Isaac's conscience against the inroads of guilt. But
this mystique is shot through with contradictions and weakness. On one hand, Faulkner has identified the wilderness
with peace, brotherhood, pity, and humility; on the other
hand, he has identified it with the primitive hunt that epito-
mizes "the will and desire to pursue and kill" (237). Although
the wilderness serves Isaac, and the seminary served Gail
Hightower, as the temple of God, they serve also as a refuge
from the world.

But there is no refuge from "the old wrong and shame" (351). This is made apparent in the last two stories of the volume, "Delta Autumn" and "Go Down, Moses." Half a century has passed; the year is 1940 now. Time was running out for both Isaac and the wilderness. The diminishing wilderness had retreated toward the Delta; it had been replaced by the plumb-ruled highways, the tremendous gins, and the "ruthless mile-wide parallelograms" (342) "of rank cotton for the frantic old-world people to turn into shells to shoot at one another" (354). Although Uncle Ike saw the advancing destruction of the woods, he seemed sustained by a benign peace, a peace bought by the repudiation of the land. Uncle Ike's gentle, Christlike peace[5] is set against signs of vague unrest and ill omen: the remote European war; the faint light and dying warmth of the tent under the constant murmuring of the rain; the sullen brooding and harsh remarks of his kinsman, the present owner of the McCaslin land, Roth Edmonds; and Will Legate's taunts about Roth's hunting of does.

The next morning Uncle Ike saw the doe. The doe was a young woman who had come in search of Roth. She was the mulatto granddaughter of Tennie's Jim, Old Carothers' Negro grandson. Roth Edmonds had committed not only miscegenation but, unwittingly, incest too—his ancestor's sin. To this woman, his own black kin, Uncle Ike cried "in that thin not loud and grieving voice: 'Get out of here! I can do nothing for you! Cant nobody do nothing for you!' " (361) His child's peace had been shattered. With quiet candor the mulatto woman reminded the shaking old man of a truth older than

---

[5] Throughout the story, "Delta Autumn," Uncle Ike is frequently (eight times) described as peaceful and untroubled. Three times he is described with his hands crossed over his breast, three times compared to a gentle child.

peace: " 'Have you lived so long and forgotten so much that you dont remember anything you ever knew or felt or even heard about love?' " (363) He was left with the wafting light and "grieving rain" (365) and his shivering body and panting breath.

No Southerner can purchase immunity. Even for an Uncle Ike there is no peace in our time. The "old wrong and shame" has not been erased, but crops up anew in different guises. Now it is the South's honor and code that deny a woman's love; now it is the North's law that executes a Negro murderer for an aborted rebellion against the white society which has rejected him—the subject of the story "Go Down, Moses." The old Negress, Aunt Mollie, is ultimately right in her lament that Roth Edmonds sold her Benjamin to Pharaoh. The execution of Butch Beauchamp began long ago with the enslavement of the Negro by the Carothers McCaslins. Now, in the twentieth century, there is still no Moses, Faulkner says, to lead the Negro out of bondage.

Go Down, Moses voices the concern of conscience over the Negro's plight in a white man's world, yet it voices too the grief of conscience over its own helplessness. The South that denies the Negro his manhood denies the white man his right to love. The power of love cannot break through the world's hard shell. Isaac McCaslin's lonely act of atonement leaves no perceptible mark upon the Southern system. As the wilderness of the old Mississippi gives way to the fields of "rank cotton for the frantic old-world people to turn into shells to shoot at one another," it becomes apparent that the evil of the old world persists in the new. There is no peace. There is only the anguish of an old man to testify to the presence of the human conscience.

11

※

Summing Up

Out of Faulkner's struggles with society and self were born the great works of his major years, 1929-1942. These works, different though they may be, are part of one man as he has responded to the stresses and dilemmas of his being and milieu. They show interrelationships, they form a pattern. It is the intention of this chapter to point up and trace that pattern—with the awareness, however, that the pattern is less "real," less significant of course, than the works. The life is in the works.

The first three novels of the period (*Sartoris, The Sound and the Fury,* and *Sanctuary*) evince a deeply rooted feeling of malaise and estrangement. They came out of a time of spiritual isolation and introspection, a time when Faulkner was completing his apprenticeship as a novelist and was still relatively unknown. His subject in these novels was the alienated self. His approach to the subject was partly skittish and evasive, partly searching and penetrating—as if he wanted and did not want to explore the roots of the aliena-tion, as if he were still embroiled in its compulsions and emo-tions.

In *Sartoris* he first became aware of the possibility of creating a world of his own, of making "men who could stand

on their hind legs and cast a long shadow." But his roman-
ticization, in different ways, of the past and present blocked
him from moving deeply into the life of the old and young
Sartorises. However romanticized and blurred, the feeling
of malaise and alienation broke through the trappings of the
sentimentalized and legendary past to provide the novel with
its principal impetus. This feeling expressed itself in young
Bayard's destructiveness and Horace Benbow's regressive-
ness. Yet since the feeling was not rooted in a specific and
credible situation, the malaise lay heavy upon the novel.
Faulkner was not quite ready then to move into the center
of the despair.

In *The Sound and the Fury* he reached into the heart of
despair and suffering. All the Compsons suffer: Benjy, Quentin, Caddy, her daughter, and even Jason. A family was falling apart and dying. But the author identified most fully
with Quentin—the sensitive, melancholy introvert unable to
cope with the present, whose obsession with his sister's chastity is symptomatic of his desire to hold tight to another time,
to a child's world. Since only an idiot can cut himself off from
time, the need to escape and withdraw becomes ultimately a
retreat to death. Working against the narcissistic and suicidal
movement of the novel is the outward thrust toward society
and life. This thrust is expressed in Jason's angry accommodation to society and Dilsey's stoic endurance, in Jason's involvement with money and Dilsey's service to the family,
in Jason's hate and Dilsey's compassion. Yet the anguish of
Quentin and the grief of Benjy over their Caddy touch every
part of the novel. The voices of Benjy, Caddy, and Quentin
interweave, as though in a fugue, with those of Jason and
Dilsey, sounding the theme of suffering and love, imparting
to *The Sound and the Fury* the feel of life itself.

In Quentin Compson the author had created his most

deeply felt portrait of an alienated, sick youth of our time; in Horace Benbow of *Sanctuary* he created an extension of Quentin, an older Quentin who chose to live and make some accommodation to society. Horace too was plagued by incestuous desire and sexual nausea; he too was sick. *Sanctuary* depicts a twentieth-century wasteland which justifies the malaise: the countryside was ravaged, the city was the home of gangsterism and prostitution, the corrupt and hypocritical ruled, and the good were powerless. Faulkner did a curious thing in this novel: he made sex—as embodied in the perverse union of Temple and Popeye, with all its destructive consequences and with its mirror image of Horace and Little Belle —the symbol of a degenerate society and of evil itself. In this way he justified Horace's aversion to sex, at the same time that he tried to reduce his own preoccupation with sex and incest. The result of this psychological disengagement and of his denigration of society is a novel characterized by surface rather than depth, by repulsion rather than understanding, and by violence rather than tragedy. Faulkner had reached a dead end in his exploration of the alienated self; he needed another subject.

He found it in the countryfolk of *As I Lay Dying*. They touched an undeveloped chord of sympathy and humor in Faulkner and led him out of the prison of self to the community of people. As in *The Sound and the Fury* he told the story of a family, but the Bundren family, despite its losses and troubles, is rooted in the earth and life. *As I Lay Dying* is a story about people; it is a fable and poem which is simply and joyously alive. Anguish gives way to comedy, despair to duty, introversion to action, and obsession to love. The mother is the source of both strength and tension and illustrates the power of love. Estranged and different from the others, she found, nevertheless, in her duty to the living a reason for staying alive. Her distrust and rejection of words sounded a fresh note in Faulkner's works and led naturally to the simple, uncomplicated Jewel, who knew only the deed and not the word. In his power to act he supplants his brother Darl. Darl is the man of words, imagination, and introspection; he tells with simple beauty the grotesque story of the Bundrens, yet he goes mad too. Like Hawthorne after his dark period of isolation, Faulkner was discovering that his salvation lay in an escape from the pit of introversion toward community with others. To become a writer he had first to cut himself off from others; to continue as a writer he had to return to them.

Light in August marked Faulkner's return to the subject of both community and isolation. Although dominated by the figures of isolation—Joanna Burden, Gail Hightower, and of course Joe Christmas—the novel conveys a new and more mature awareness of society and community, a recognition that, willy or nilly, man is in and of society. These solitary figures are seen in terms of their society. In fact, the central question raised by the book is what happens to man who cannot relate to his society, who cannot relate to any living creature? How does he achieve identity? How does he become human? Joe Christmas is the incarnation of alienation; whatever identity he possesses derives from his rejection of and by others. But such an identity—and this is true of Hightower and Miss Burden too—is depicted as warped and incomplete. All three are so dehumanized by isolation that they turn from life to death. To recover life one must find one's way back to the nature of being, to that which is and needs not know why—to a Lena Grove. To hold on to Lena Grove becomes the task of the Southern countryman, Byron Bunch. But in a South obsessed and divided by the racial issue, in a South shaped and often dominated by the Simon

McEacherns, Doc Hineses, and Percy Grimms, it is hard to hold on to the quiet sanity of simple existence and natural being. *Light in August* was Faulkner's first full-scale work to deal with the effect of the Negro on the Southern mind and conscience.

In *Absalom, Absalom!* Faulkner continued to move toward greater social involvement—converting his own innerness, malaise, and estrangement into a social conscience. In his search and struggle to understand the South, he journeyed back to its past. He had to re-create the past out of bits of talk and anecdotes, conjecture and legends, intuition and imagination; he had to do it in spite of conflicting loyalties. The center and nexus of the legends and loyalties was the Old South as embodied in the planter-aristocrats; they were the makers of the South, its giants and heroes. Now one of their descendants in the twentieth century was struggling to write about them, knowing full well that he was not like them, that he was one of those who could not do and who, suffering because he could not do, had to write.[1] So he wrote about the black and white families of Thomas Sutpen, about the father who was not a father, the son who was not a son, and the brothers who destroyed one another. He wrote about the sin and its retribution. He wrote out of an overwrought imagination and afflicted heart and aggrieved conscience, for these were his people and the South was his home. He wrote what he had to write.

But when Faulkner tried to deal with the Civil War and Reconstruction period in the volume of stories about the

---

[1] These words are a paraphrase of a passage in *The Unvanquished* which tells of the thoughts of Colonel Sartoris' son at a time when he was struggling to find his own way: ". . . I realised then the immitigable chasm between all life and all print—that those who can, do, those who cannot and suffer enough because they can't, write about it." *The Unvanquished* (New York, Random House, 1938), p.262.

Sartorises entitled *The Unvanquished*, he presented another
version of the South: sentimental, superficial, and stereotyped. Apparently there were two Faulkners: the writer who
produced for the *Saturday Evening Post*, and the artist who
created the tragic *Absalom, Absalom!*; the Southerner whose
historical view was shaped by legend and wishful thinking,
and the Southerner who broke through the defenses and
illusions to reach the truth that resided in the heart and
conscience. However, in the last story, "An Odor of Verbena,"
the artist once more emerged. Its drama rests in the clash
between the son and father. Rejecting his father's way of
honor and violence, Bayard turned, in a sense, from Cain to
Christ. Unlike his father, he could not become a leader of
his people, but he could express, in his own small way, the
buried conscience of the South.

In Faulkner's next book, *The Wild Palms,* he departed the
familiar world of Yoknapatawpha for strange territory. The
romance of Harry Wilbourne and Charlotte Rittenmeyer
took him from New Orleans to Chicago to Utah and finally
to a coastal town in Mississippi. Although the subject, as
well as the territory, seemed strange for Faulkner, he was
returning to an old theme: love between man and woman.
He struggled in the story of Charlotte and Wilbourne to overcome his antipathy toward sex and to present sex as a natural
element of love; the result was a curiously flat, depressive
romance. He was at ease only when telling the story of the
convict and the pregnant woman. Their relationship—with
the woman living as mother, the man as protector—was a
natural one for Faulkner; the other was not. Evolving from
the two stories of two kinds of love was the primitivistic thesis
that middle-class civilization was imprisoning and warping
natural man and destroying life itself. Faulkner's hostility
toward the middle-class world underlay the rationale of the

thesis, and this hostility merged, as in *The Sound and the Fury* and *Sanctuary*, with his antipathy to sex.

Just as Faulkner had turned from the obsession and malaise of *The Sound and the Fury* and *Sanctuary* (first version) to the countryfolk of *As I Lay Dying*, so did he turn with the writing of *The Hamlet* to the small farmers of Frenchman's Bend. The slow rhythm, easy humor, and simplicity of their life provided him with a subject which seemed free from the morbid preoccupation of his early works. Instead of Caddy, there was Eula; instead of Quentin, Jody; instead of Mr. Compson, Will Varner; and instead of Popeye and Temple or Wilbourne and Charlotte, there were the idiot and his cow. An earthy, fantastic comic spirit was taking over, transforming distress into laughter and bringing everything down to earth. Sharing in this spirit and adding his own benign sanity was the ubiquitous and irrepressible Ratliff. Yet the comic spirit, even in the country owned by Will Varner and tended by Ratliff, could not fully prevail. The stories of Labove's passion for Eula and of the idiot's devotion to his cow introduce a tense, pathetic quality that breaks with the mood of comedy. The coming of Flem Snopes to Frenchman's Bend, though it brings some excitement, brings also a threat to the hamlet's way of life—a new kind of acquisitiveness; nevertheless, in final analysis, Flem's rise to power is depicted as more comic than tragic. What really darkens the comic spirit is the story of Mink Snopes. In this harassed and tough little sharecropper Faulkner caught the bleakness and hopelessness of the sharecropper's existence, but he caught too a resistance, a pride, an indomitability. Faulkner managed in the various stories of *The Hamlet* to fuse their discrete, discordant qualities: pathos with terror, outrage with hilarity, poetic fantasy with earthy realism, and comedy with tragedy. Brilliantly transforming his preoccupation through his comic genius and bringing to life the people for whom he had such a special regard and understanding, he created his own kind of tragicomedy.

In *Go Down, Moses* and, more particularly, in "The Bear," Faulkner circled back to old themes, metamorphosing them in the process of developing further his concern with the Negro and the South. He was writing, in a sense, about love. It was the kind of love that had moved him deeply in the writing of *The Sound and the Fury*, for it was based upon the innocence and natural affection of childhood and created a world for which the protagonist longed at the very time he knew how irrecoverable it was. In *The Sound and the Fury* the child's world where brother could love sister had been blighted by the curse of sexuality; in *Go Down, Moses* the child's world where black and white could live as brothers was destroyed by the curse of the South—racism. The difference in the two curses, as well as the difference in the two protagonists (Quentin Compson and Isaac McCaslin), indicates the change in Faulkner's concern and outlook over the span of thirteen years. Isaac is a variation of Quentin: he is a guilt-ridden idealist whose guilt is that of a troubled nation, whereas Quentin's is that of a troubled youth. Isaac is also an extension of Bayard Sartoris of *The Unvanquished*, another Christlike dissenter who breaks with the Southern code. Isaac embodies the ambivalent tensions of the sensitive, decent Southerner who wishes to atone for the sin against the Negro but who finds himself helpless to make any change in the system. In the face of an apparently insoluble dilemma Quentin chose death, but Isaac chooses life, though in such attenuated form that he too seems to retreat from his dilemma. Isaac's refuge is the wilderness, which Faulkner beautifully renders into the symbol of a golden age before man had surrendered to the curse of possession. But, like the child's world, the wilderness is destroyed.

The author of these works seemed to be reaching in the midst of evil or malaise for a simpler and more decent life, for simpler and more decent people. In *Sartoris* there were the MacCallum family, in *The Sound and the Fury* Dilsey, in *As I Lay Dying* Jewel and Cash Bundren, in *Light in August* Byron Bunch and Lena Grove, in *The Wild Palms* the tall convict, in *The Hamlet* Ratliff, and in *Go Down, Moses* Sam Fathers; and always there were the children and the idiots. Part of the author seemed to be seeking love uncorrupted by lust, simplicity rather than complexity, innocence rather than guilt, strength and integration in place of weakness and fragmentation, and the will to live instead of the desire to die. Yet the other part of him, ironically and despairingly, was aware of the reality which made a mockery of hopes and ideals.

That Faulkner's reality is almost always an extreme of the human condition testifies in one sense to his outraged awareness of the gap between the ideal and the actuality, but it testifies in another sense to the extremity of his own condition. With Faulkner, as with all men, the personal condition underlay and shaped his view of the human condition. In his early works (1929-1932), where the subject is close to his personal situation, the tension and despair tend to override the material but invest it with a powerful immediacy and urgency. The style of the early Faulkner seems to evolve simply and naturally from the intensity of his emotion and the brooding of his imagination. Generally the language has purity, concreteness, and aptness; it is an organic part of the deeply felt and truly created life.

But the style of the later works changes. The prose has become baroque and strained, the approach oblique, the feelings obscured and attenuated. The sentences seem to unwind from an endless spool, the writing to take on a stylized, compulsive quality. A tired, nagging fury seems to drive the author; behind the fury there is despair, as if he felt the futility of the words he could not stop writing, as if writing itself were becoming but a desperate means of suspending reality. In general *The Sound and the Fury, As I Lay Dying,* and *Light in August* move in on life; *Absalom, Absalom!, The Wild Palms,* and "The Bear" move away from life. The will to confront reality seems to be losing out to the need to escape. Concentration yields to diffusiveness; for example, not just the style but the very structure of *The Unvanquished, The Wild Palms, The Hamlet,* and *Go Down, Moses* exhibits this diffusiveness. The oblique approach and turgid prose of the late work reflect an evasiveness as well as a more complex involvement with the subject—complex not only because of the increasing ambivalence but because of the fragmentation of the author's emotions. To say this is not to deny the genius of *Absalom, The Hamlet,* and "The Bear" but to recognize a significant change in its expression and to suggest that its hard fire is beginning to burn out.[2]

That the genius of the American writer is short-lived and tends to concentrate itself in a single work (like *The Scarlet Letter, Moby-Dick, Huckleberry Finn,* and *The Red Badge*

---

[2] This decline is much more perceptible in the works that follow *Go Down, Moses.* However, as if to compensate for their failure to do justice to the genius of the early Faulkner, critics have tended to overpraise his works of the forties and fifties. One of the exceptions has been Irving Howe, who has commented in this way: "Though the novels he wrote in the forties and fifties contain many fine and even brilliant parts, they are on the whole forced, anxious and high-pitched, the work of a man, no longer driven, who now drives himself. . . . In all these works there is a reliance upon a high-powered rhetoric which bears the outer marks of the earlier Faulkner style, but is really a kind of self-imitation, a whipped-up fury pouring out in wanton excess. There is a tendency to fall back upon hi-jinks of plot, a flaunting arbitrariness and whimsicality of invention—as if Faulkner, wearied of telling stories and establishing characters, were now deliberately breaking his own spell and betraying an impatience with his own skill." See "End of a Road," *New Republic,* 141 (Dec. 7, 1959), 17-18.

of Courage) has become practically an American tradition. However fiercely the flame of the American genius may burn, it burns out quickly. This seems true of Fitzgerald and Hemingway too, but less so of Faulkner. Faulkner has produced a greater quantity and variety of first-rate work than any American writer, with the exception of Henry James. Consider, for example, *The Sound and the Fury, As I Lay Dying, Light in August, Absalom, The Hamlet,* and "The Bear." Such an accomplishment is of the first order. Yet in some ways the generalization does apply. Faulkner has concentrated the essence of what he has had to say in one superb novel, *The Sound and the Fury.* In one way or another, the rest of his novels and stories rework, often brilliantly and enigmatically, the themes of that novel.

Nostalgia and flight, Wright Morris has observed, are central to American life and literature: the American flees the raw and uncongenial present for a mythic and desired past.[3] These themes are central to the works of Faulkner too. Almost all his protagonists—Bayard Sartoris (*Sartoris*), Quentin Compson, Horace Benbow, Joe Christmas, Charles and Valery Bon, Harry Wilbourne, and Isaac McCaslin— are in flight from a present which is too much with them. Some, like Christmas and Wilbourne, have nothing to cherish or turn back to; but others, like Quentin and Isaac, look back to another time, a golden age of innocence and love. That the idyll may never have existed as imagined or remembered is not really the point; it exists to give voice to a present need. The need is love. The love is located in the past, in childhood; and its foes are located in the present, in society and sex.

---

[3] Wright Morris, *The Territory Ahead* (New York, Atheneum, 1963), 24-26, 41-44.

Like the Frenchmen of the Second World War generation, Faulkner and his class were born into a world which, having dispossessed them of their former power and glory, had now relegated them to a minor role. Circumstance bred in them both a proud resistance and a despairing defeatism. The brutality and ignominy of the present forced them, in their need to hold on to some sustaining pride, to look backward to past glories. But as Faulkner looked more deeply into the Southern past, he found the same kind of evil which oppressed him in the present. The only past he could still believe in was that of childhood, when the family had made a separate world of its own, insulated from the outside world by its innocence and completeness. That was the time when love was still love, when one's response was still human.

Like many Southern writers from Mark Twain to Carson McCullers, Faulkner was seeking to preserve some quality of the child that the adult world destroyed. Particularly for the twentieth-century Southern writer, the recoil from society has been sharp, driving the author inward into self and backward to the child or the grotesque. There is in these writers a new note of anguish, a greater sense of the wrenching and deforming of the human heart. Yet much more than many Southern writers, Faulkner remained a part of his people—at one with them in their simple joys and tragedies, apart from them in their failure to recognize the needs of the heart, black and white. Faulkner's works convey a deep sense of oppression and withdrawal, yet they convey too the struggle with self and society. In the midst of defeat and despair a small center of resistance resides. From this resistance and from an anguished heart Faulkner has cried out against whatever oppresses the human spirit.

Selected Bibliography

WORKS BY FAULKNER

The Marble Faun (Poems). Boston: The Four Seas, 1924. Random House Edition (with *A Green Bough*), 1965.

Soldiers' Pay (Novel). New York: Boni and Liveright, 1926.

Mosquitoes (Novel). New York: Boni and Liveright, 1927.

Sartoris (Novel). New York: Harcourt, Brace, 1929. Random House Edition, 1956.

The Sound and the Fury (Novel). New York: Cape and Smith, 1929. Modern Library Edition (with *As I Lay Dying*), 1946.

As I Lay Dying (Novel). New York: Cape and Smith, 1930. Modern Library Edition (with *The Sound and the Fury*), 1946.

Sanctuary (Novel). New York: Cape and Smith, 1931. Modern Library Edition, 1932.

These 13 (Stories). New York: Cape and Smith, 1931.

Light in August (Novel). New York: Harrison Smith and Robert Haas, 1932. Modern Library Edition, 1950.

A Green Bough (Poems). New York: Smith and Haas, 1933. Random House Edition (with *The Marble Faun*), 1965.

Doctor Martino and Other Stories (Stories). New York: Smith and Haas, 1934.

Pylon (Novel). New York: Smith and Haas, 1935. Random House Edition, 1965.

Absalom, Absalom! (Novel). New York: Random House, 1936. Modern Library Edition, 1951.

The Unvanquished (Novel). New York: Random House, 1938.

The Wild Palms (Novel). New York: Random House, 1939.

The Hamlet (Novel). New York: Random House, 1940.

Go Down, Moses and Other Stories (Novel). New York: Ran-

dom House, 1942. Reissued in a Modern Library Edition in
1955 as *Go Down, Moses*.

Intruder in the Dust (Novel). New York: Random House, 1948.

Knight's Gambit (Stories). New York: Random House, 1949.

Collected Stories of William Faulkner (Stories). New York: Random House, 1950.

Requiem for a Nun (Novel). New York: Random House, 1951.

A Fable (Novel). New York: Random House, 1954.

Big Woods (Stories). New York: Random House, 1955.

The Town (Novel). New York: Random House, 1957.

The Mansion (Novel). New York: Random House, 1959.

The Reivers (Novel). New York: Random House, 1962.

Selected Short Stories of William Faulkner (Stories). New York: Modern Library, 1962.

SELECTED STORIES

The following is a list of Faulkner stories referred to in this text
and/or used by him in writing *The Unvanquished, The Hamlet*,
or *Go Down, Moses*.

"A Rose for Emily," *Forum*, 83 (April 1930), 233-238. Reprinted,
somewhat revised, in *These 13* and *Collected Stories*.

"Dry September," *Scribner's*, 89 (Jan. 1931), 49-56. Revised
version in *These 13* and *Collected Stories*.

"That Evening Sun Go Down," *American Mercury*, 22 (March
1931), 257-267. Revised and re-entitled "That Evening Sun"
in *These 13* and *Collected Stories*.

"Hair," *American Mercury*, 23 (May 1931), 53-61. Revised version in *These 13* and *Collected Stories*.

"Spotted Horses," *Scribner's*, 89 (June 1931), 585-597. Incorporated and extensively revised in *The Hamlet*.

"The Hound," *Harper's*, 163 (Aug. 1931), 266-274. Reprinted
in *Doctor Martino;* incorporated and extensively revised in
The Hamlet.

"Carcassonne," *These 13*, pp.352-358. Reprinted in *Collected Stories*.

"Lizards in Jamshyd's Courtyard," *Saturday Evening Post*, 204
(Feb. 27, 1932), 12-13, 52, 57. Incorporated and revised in
The Hamlet.

"Wash," *Harper's*, 168 (Feb. 1934), 258-266. Reprinted in *Doctor Martino* and *Collected Stories;* incorporated and revised in *Absalom, Absalom!*.

"Ambuscade," *Saturday Evening Post*, 207 (Sept. 29, 1934), 12-13, 80, 81. Revised in *The Unvanquished*.

"Retreat," *Saturday Evening Post*, 207 (Oct. 13, 1934), 16-17, 82, 84, 85, 87, 89. Revised in *The Unvanquished*.

"Lo!" *Story*, 5 (Nov. 1934), 5-21. Reprinted in *Collected Stories*.

"Raid," *Saturday Evening Post*, 207 (Nov. 3, 1934), 18-19, 72, 73, 75, 77-78. Revised in *The Unvanquished*.

"Skirmish at Sartoris," *Scribner's*, 97 (April 1935), 193-200. Revised in *The Unvanquished*.

"Lion," *Harper's*, 172 (Dec. 1935), 67-77. Extensively revised and incorporated in "The Bear," *Go Down, Moses*.

"Fool About a Horse," *Scribner's*, 100 (Aug. 1936), 80-86. Revised and incorporated in *The Hamlet*.

"The Unvanquished," *Saturday Evening Post*, 209 (Nov. 14, 1936), 12-13, 121, 122, 124, 126, 128, 130. Revised and entitled "Riposte in Tertio" in *The Unvanquished*.

"Vendée," *Saturday Evening Post*, 209 (Dec. 5, 1936), 16-17, 86, 87, 90, 92, 93, 94. Revised in *The Unvanquished*.

"Barn Burning," *Harper's*, 179 (June 1939), 86-96. Reprinted in *Collected Stories*. The material is partly used in *The Hamlet*.

"A Point of Law," *Collier's*, 105 (June 22, 1940), 20-21, 30, 32. Revised and incorporated in "The Fire and the Hearth," *Go Down, Moses*.

"The Old People," *Harper's*, 181 (Sept. 1940), 418-425. Revised in *Go Down, Moses* and *Big Woods*.

"Pantaloon in Black," *Harper's*, 181 (Oct. 1940), 503-513. Revised in *Go Down, Moses*.

"Gold Is Not Always," *Atlantic*, 166 (Nov. 1940), 563-570. Revised and incorporated in "The Fire and the Hearth," *Go Down, Moses*.

"Go Down, Moses," *Collier's*, 107 (Jan. 25, 1941), 19-20, 45, 46. Revised in *Go Down, Moses*.

"The Bear," *Saturday Evening Post*, 214 (May 9, 1942), 30-31, 74, 76, 77. This is a highly abridged version of "The Bear" in *Go Down, Moses and Other Stories* (published May 11, 1942).

The *Go Down, Moses* version, except for the fourth section, has been reprinted in *Big Woods*.

"L'Après-midi d'une Vache," *Fontaine*, 27-28 (June-July 1943), 66-81 (translated by Maurice Edgar Coindreau). Original English version published in *Furioso*, 2 (Summer 1947), 5-17 (under the pseudonym of Ernest V. Trueblood).

COLLECTIONS OF WORKS AND INTERVIEWS

The Portable Faulkner. Malcolm Cowley, ed. New York: The Viking Press, 1946.

The Faulkner Reader. Saxe Commins, ed. New York: Random House, 1954.

Faulkner at Nagano. Robert A. Jelliffe, ed. Tokyo: Kenkyusha Press, 1956.

William Faulkner: New Orleans Sketches. Carvel Collins, ed. New Brunswick, N. J.: Rutgers University Press, 1958. Evergreen Edition, New York: Grove, 1961.

Faulkner in the University. Frederick L. Gwynn and Joseph L. Blotner, eds. Charlottesville: University of Virginia Press, 1959. Vintage Edition, New York: Random House, 1965.

William Faulkner: Early Prose and Poetry. Carvel Collins, ed. Boston: Little, Brown, 1962.

Faulkner at West Point. Joseph L. Fant, III, and Robert Ashley, eds. New York: Random House, 1964.

BIBLIOGRAPHY

Meriwether, James B. "William Faulkner: A Check List," *Princeton University Library Chronicle*, 18 (Spring 1957), 136-158. A bibliography of Faulkner's works.

Vickery, Olga W. "A Selective Bibliography," *William Faulkner: Three Decades of Criticism*. East Lansing: Michigan State University Press, 1960. Pp.393-428. A bibliography of Faulkner criticism.

Sleeth, Irene Lynn. "William Faulkner: A Bibliography of Criticism," *Twentieth Century Literature*, 8 (April 1962), 18-43. Also published separately in The Swallow Pamphlets, Number 13. Denver: Alan Swallow, 1962.

BOOKS ON FAULKNER

Beck, Warren. *Man in Motion: Faulkner's Trilogy.* Madison: University of Wisconsin Press, 1961.

Blotner, Joseph. *William Faulkner's Library—A Catalogue.* Charlottesville: University of Virginia Press, 1964.

Brooks, Cleanth. *William Faulkner: The Yoknapatawpha Country.* New Haven: Yale University Press, 1963.

Campbell, Harry Modean and Ruel E. Foster. *William Faulkner: A Critical Appraisal.* Norman: University of Oklahoma Press, 1951.

Coughlan, Robert. *The Private World of William Faulkner.* New York: Harper, 1954.

Cullen, John B. in collaboration with Floyd C. Watkins. *Old Times in the Faulkner Country.* Chapel Hill: University of North Carolina Press, 1961.

Dain, Martin J. *Faulkner's County—Yoknapatawpha* (Photos taken in and around Oxford, Mississippi). New York: Random House, 1964.

Faulkner, John. *My Brother Bill: An Affectionate Reminiscence.* New York: Trident Press, 1963.

Ford, Margaret P. and Suzanne Kincaid. *Who's Who in Faulkner.* Baton Rouge: Louisiana State University Press, 1963.

Hoffman, Frederick J. *William Faulkner.* New York: Twayne, 1961.

————and Olga W. Vickery, eds. *William Faulkner: Two Decades of Criticism.* East Lansing: Michigan State College Press, 1951.

————. *William Faulkner: Three Decades of Criticism.* East Lansing: Michigan State University Press, 1960.

Howe, Irving. *William Faulkner: A Critical Study.* New York: Random House, 1952. Second edition revised and expanded in Vintage Books, 1962.

Hunt, John W. *William Faulkner: Art in Theological Tension.* Syracuse: Syracuse University Press, 1965.

Kirk, Robert W. and Marvin Klotz. *Faulkner's People.* Berkeley and Los Angeles: University of California Press, 1963.

Longley, John Lewis, Jr. *The Tragic Mask: A Study of Faulkner's Heroes.* Chapel Hill: University of North Carolina Press, 1963.

Malin, Irving. *William Faulkner: An Interpretation*. Stanford: Stanford University Press, 1957.

Meriwether, James B. *The Literary Career of William Faulkner: A Bibliographical Study*. Princeton: Princeton University Library, 1961.

Millgate, Michael. *William Faulkner*. New York: Grove, 1961.

———. *Achievement of William Faulkner*. New York: Random House, 1966.

Miner, Ward L. *The World of William Faulkner*. Durham, N. C.: Duke University Press, 1952.

Nilon, Charles H. *Faulkner and the Negro*. (University of Colorado Studies: Series in Language and Literature, No. 8.) Boulder: University of Colorado Press, September 1962.

O'Connor, William Van. *The Tangled Fire of William Faulkner*. Minneapolis: University of Minnesota Press, 1954.

———. *William Faulkner*. (Pamphlets on American Writers, No. 3). Minneapolis: University of Minnesota Press, 1959.

Robb, Mary Cooper. *William Faulkner: An Estimate of His Contribution to the American Novel*. Pittsburgh: University of Pittsburgh Press, 1957.

Runyan, Harry. *A Faulkner Glossary*. New York: Citadel, 1964.

Slatoff, Walter J. *Quest for Failure: A Study of William Faulkner*. Ithaca: Cornell University Press, 1960.

Swiggart, Peter. *The Art of Faulkner's Novels*. Austin: University of Texas Press, 1962.

Thompson, Lawrence. *William Faulkner: An Introduction and Interpretation*. New York: Barnes & Noble, 1963.

Tuck, Dorothy. *Crowell's Handbook of Faulkner*. New York: Crowell, 1964.

Utley, Francis Lee, Lynn Z. Bloom, and Arthur F. Kinney (eds.). *Bear, Man, and God: Seven Approaches to William Faulkner's "The Bear."* New York: Random House, 1964.

Vickery, Olga W. *The Novels of William Faulkner: A Critical Interpretation*. Baton Rouge: Louisiana State University Press, 1959.

Volpe, Edmond L. *A Reader's Guide to William Faulkner*. New York: Noonday, 1964.

Waggoner, Hyatt H. *William Faulkner: From Jefferson to the World*. Lexington: University of Kentucky Press, 1959.

Webb, James W. and A. Wigfall Green, eds. *William Faulkner of Oxford*. Baton Rouge: Louisiana State University Press, 1965.

BOOKS ON THE BACKGROUND

Baldwin, Joseph G. *The Flush Times of Alabama and Mississippi*. New York: D. Appleton & Co., 1853. New York: Hill & Wang, 1957.

Bancroft, Frederick. *Slave Trading in the Old South*. Baltimore: J. H. Furst Co., 1931. New York: Frederick Ungar, 1959.

Cash, W. J. *The Mind of the South*. New York: Knopf, 1941. Garden City, N. Y.: Doubleday, 1954.

Craven, Avery. *The Coming of the Civil War*. New York: Scribner's, 1950.

―――. *The Growth of Southern Nationalism, 1848-1861*. Baton Rouge: Louisiana State University Press, 1953.

Douglass, Frederick. *Narrative of the Life of Frederick Douglass, an American Slave, Written by Himself*, ed. Benjamin Quarles. Cambridge: Belknap, 1960. Originally published in Boston, 1845.

DuBois, W. E. Burghardt. *Black Folk: Then and Now*. New York: Holt, 1939.

Duclos, Donald Philip. *Son of Sorrow: The Life, Works and Influence of Colonel William C. Falkner, 1825-1889*. University of Michigan Doctoral Dissertation, 1961 (Microfilmed in 1962).

Dyer, G. W. *Democracy in the South Before the Civil War*. Nashville: Methodist Episcopal Church, South, 1905.

Elkins, Stanley M. *Slavery*. Chicago: University of Chicago Press, 1959.

Franklin, John Hope. *From Slavery to Freedom*. New York: Knopf, 1952.

Frazier, E. Franklin. *The Negro Family in the United States*. New York: Dryden, 1948.

Hickerson, Thomas Felix. *The Falkner Feuds*. Chapel Hill: Colonial Press, 1964.

Lewis, R. W. B. *The American Adam: Innocence, Tragedy and Tradition in the Nineteenth Century*. Chicago: University of Chicago Press, 1955.

Mannix, Daniel P. in collaboration with Malcolm Cowley. *Black Cargoes: A History of the Atlantic Slave Trade.* New York: Viking, 1962.

Morris, Wright. *The Territory Ahead.* New York: Harcourt, Brace, 1958. New York: Atheneum, 1963.

Myrdal, Gunnar (with assistance of Richard Sterner and Arnold Rose). *An American Dilemma: The Negro Problem and Modern Democracy.* New York: Harper, 1944.

Odum, Howard W. *The Way of the South.* New York: Macmillan, 1947.

Olmsted, Frederick Law. *A Journey in the Seaboard Slave States, with Remarks on Their Economy.* New York: Dix & Edwards, 1856.

————. *A Journey in the Back Country.* New York: Mason Brothers, 1860.

Owsley, Frank Lawrence. *Plain Folk of the Old South.* Baton Rouge: Louisiana State University Press, 1949.

Rourke, Constance. *American Humor: A Study of the National Character.* New York: Harcourt, Brace, 1931. Garden City, N. Y.: Doubleday, 1953.

Smith, Henry Nash. *Virgin Land: The American West as Symbol and Myth.* Cambridge: Harvard University Press, 1950. Vintage Edition in 1957.

Sydnor, Charles Sackett. *Slavery in Mississippi.* New York: Appleton-Century, 1933.

Tannenbaum, Frank. *Slave and Citizen: The Negro in the Americas.* New York: Knopf, 1947.

Taylor, William R. *Cavalier and Yankee.* New York: Braziller, 1961.

Tocqueville, Alexis de. *Democracy in America.* 2 vols. Edited by Phillips Bradley. New York: Knopf, 1946.

Turner, Frederick Jackson. *The Frontier in American History.* New York: Henry Holt, 1920.

Weaver, Herbert. *Mississippi Farmers, 1850-1860.* Nashville, Tenn.: Vanderbilt University Press, 1945.

Wertenbaker, Thomas Jefferson. *Patrician and Plebeian in Virginia.* Charlottesville, Virginia: Privately printed, 1910. New York: Russell & Russell, 1958.

Wharton, Vernon Lane. *The Negro in Mississippi, 1865-1890.*
Chapel Hill: University of North Carolina Press, 1947.
Woodward, C. Vann. *Origins of the New South, 1877-1913.* Baton
Rouge: Louisiana State University Press, 1951.
————. *The Strange Career of Jim Crow.* New York: Oxford
(Galaxy Edition), 1957. The Galaxy Edition is a revised and
enlarged edition of *The Strange Career of Jim Crow* copy-
righted by Oxford University Press in 1955 and first delivered
in 1954 at the University of Virginia as the James W. Richard
Lectures in History.
————. *The Burden of Southern History.* Baton Rouge: Louisiana
State University Press, 1960. New York: Vintage Edition.

ARTICLES—CRITICAL AND BIOGRAPHICAL

The following is a list of articles referred to in this study.

Blum, Irving D. "The Parallel Philosophy of Emerson's 'Nature'
and Faulkner's 'The Bear'," *Emerson Society Quarterly,* No.
13 (4th Quarter, 1958), 22-25.
Brown, Andrew. "The First Mississippi Partisan Rangers, C.S.A.,"
Civil War History, I (Dec. 1955), 371-399.
Brown, Maud Morrow. "William C. Falkner, Man of Legends,"
Georgia Review, 10 (Winter 1956), 421-438.
Brumm, Ursula. "Wilderness and Civilization: A Note on Wil-
liam Faulkner," *Partisan Review,* 22 (Summer 1955), 340-350.
Cantwell, Robert. "The Faulkners: Recollections of a Gifted
Family," *New World Writing* (Second Mentor Selection,
1952), 300-315.
————. Introduction to William C. Falkner's *The White Rose of
Memphis* (New York: Coley Taylor, 1953), v-xxvii.
Chase, Richard. "Faulkner—The Great Years," in his *The Ameri-
can Novel and Its Tradition.* Garden City, N. Y.: Doubleday,
1957. Pp.205-241.
Collins, Carvel. "About the Sketches," Introduction to *William
Faulkner: New Orleans Sketches.* New Brunswick, N.J.: Rut-
gers University Press, 1958. Pp.9-34.
Cowley, Malcolm. "Introduction to *The Portable Faulkner,*" *Wil-
liam Faulkner: Three Decades of Criticism.* East Lansing: Mich-

igan State University Press, 1960. Pp.94-109. Originally published in *The Portable Faulkner*. New York: Viking, 1946. Pp.
1-24.

————. "Go Down to Faulkner's Land," *The New Republic*, 106
(June 29, 1942), 900.

Douglas, Harold J. and Robert Daniel. "Faulkner and the Puritanism of the South," *Tennessee Studies in Literature*, 2
(1957), 6-10.

Farmer, Norman J. "The Love Theme: A Principal Source of
Thematic Unity in Faulkner's Snopes Trilogy," *Twentieth Century Literature*, 8 (Oct. 1962-Jan. 1963), 111-123.

Greet, T. Y. "The Theme and Structure of Faulkner's *The Hamlet*," *William Faulkner: Three Decades of Criticism*. East Lansing: Michigan State University Press, 1960. Pp.330-347.
Originally published in *PMLA*, 72 (Sept. 1957), 775-790.

Gwynn, Frederick L. "Faulkner's Raskolnikov," *Modern Fiction
Studies*, 4 (Summer 1958), 169-172.

Handy, William J. "*As I Lay Dying:* Faulkner's Inner Reporter,"
Kenyon Review, 21 (Summer 1959), 437-451.

Holman, C. Hugh. "The Unity of Faulkner's *Light in August*,"
PMLA, 73 (March 1958), 155-166.

Hopkins, Viola. "Meaning and Form in Faulkner's *The Hamlet*,"
Accent, 15 (Spring 1955), 125-144.

Howe, Irving. "End of a Road," *New Republic*, 141 (Dec. 7,
1959), 17-21.

Kazin, Alfred. "The Stillness of *Light in August*," *William Faulk-
ner: Three Decades of Criticism*. East Lansing: Michigan State
University Press, 1960. Pp.247-265. Originally published in
Twelve Original Essays on Great American Novels, ed. Charles
Shapiro. Detroit: Wayne State University Press, 1958. Pp.257-
283.

Kubie, Lawrence S. "William Faulkner's *Sanctuary:* An Analysis,"
Saturday Review of Literature, 11 (Oct. 20, 1934), 218, 224-
226.

LaBudde, Kenneth. "Cultural Primitivism in William Faulkner's
'The Bear'," *American Quarterly*, 2 (Winter 1950), 322-328.

Levine, Paul. "Love and Money in the Snopes Trilogy," *College
English*, 23 (Dec. 1961), 196-199.

Lewis, R. W. B. "The Hero in the New World: William Faulkner's 'The Bear'," *Kenyon Review*, 13 (Autumn 1951), 641-660. Reprinted in several works, e.g., *Interpretations of American Literature*, Charles Feidelson, Jr. and Paul Brodtkorb, Jr. (eds.). New York: Oxford, 1959. Pp.332-349.

Lind, Ilse Dusoir. "The Design and Meaning of *Absalom, Absalom!*" *William Faulkner: Three Decades of Criticism*. East Lansing: Michigan State University Press, 1960. Pp.278-304. Originally published in *PMLA*, 70 (Dec. 1955), 887-912.

————. "The Calvinistic Burden of *Light in August*," *New England Quarterly* 30 (Sept. 1957), 307-329.

Lisca, Peter. "*The Hamlet*: Genesis and Revisions," *Faulkner Studies*, 3 (Spring 1954), 5-13.

Longley, John L. "Joe Christmas: The Hero in the Modern World," *William Faulkner: Three Decades of Criticism*. East Lansing: Michigan State University Press, 1960. Pp.265-278. Originally published in *Virginia Quarterly Review*, 33 (Spring 1957), 233-249.

Massey, Linton. "Notes on the Unrevised Galleys of Faulkner's *Sanctuary*," *Studies in Bibliography*, 8 (1956), 195-208.

Meriwether, James B. "Some Notes on the Text of Faulkner's *Sanctuary*," *Papers of the Bibliographical Society of America*, 55 (Third Quarter, 1961), 192-206.

Moldenhauer, Joseph J. "Unity of Theme and Structure in *The Wild Palms*," *William Faulkner: Three Decades of Criticism*. East Lansing: Michigan State University Press, 1960. Pp.305-322.

Moses, W. R. "Where History Crosses Myth: Another Reading of 'The Bear'," *Accent*, 13 (Winter 1953), 21-33.

————. "The Unity of *The Wild Palms*," *Modern Fiction Studies*, 2 (Autumn 1956), 125-131.

————. "Water, Water Everywhere: *Old Man* and *A Farewell to Arms*," *Modern Fiction Studies*, 5 (Summer 1959), 172-174.

O'Connor, William Van. "The Wilderness Theme in Faulkner's 'The Bear'," *Accent*, 13 (Winter 1953), 12-20.

———— "Hawthorne and Faulkner: Some Common Ground," *Virginia Quarterly Review*, 33 (Winter 1957), 105-123.

O'Donnell, George Marion. "Faulkner's Mythology," *William*

Faulkner: Three Decades of Criticism. East Lansing: Michigan State University Press, 1960. Pp.82-93. Originally published in *Kenyon Review,* 1 (Summer 1939), 285-299.

O'Faolain, Sean. "William Faulkner, or More Genius Than Talent," in his *The Vanishing Hero: Studies in Novelists of the Twenties.* London: Eyre and Spottiswoode, 1956. Pp.100-134.

Perluck, Herbert A. " 'The Heart's Driving Complexity': An Unromantic Reading of Faulkner's 'The Bear'," *Accent,* 20 (Winter 1960), 23-46.

Richardson, H. Edward. "The 'Hemingwaves' in Faulkner's *The Wild Palms," Modern Fiction Studies,* 4 (Winter 1958-1959), 357-360.

Roscoe, Lavon. "An Interview with William Faulkner," *Western Review,* 15 (Summer 1951), 300-304.

Sewall, Richard B. *"Absalom, Absalom!"* in his *The Vision of Tragedy.* New Haven, Conn.: Yale University Press, 1959. Pp.133-147.

Slabey, Robert M. "Joe Christmas, Faulkner's Marginal Man," *Phylon,* 21 (Fall 1960), 266-277.

Stein, Jean. "William Faulkner: An Interview," *William Faulkner: Three Decades of Criticism.* East Lansing: Michigan State University Press, 1960. Pp.67-81. Originally published in *Paris Review,* 4 (Spring 1956), 28-52.

Stewart, Randall. "Hawthorne and Faulkner," *College English,* 17 (Feb. 1956), 258-262.

————. "The Vision of Evil in Hawthorne and Faulkner," in *The Tragic Vision and the Christian Faith,* ed. Nathan A. Scott, Jr. New York: Association Press, 1957. Pp.238-263.

Sullivan, Walter. "The Tragic Design of *Absalom, Absalom!" South Atlantic Quarterly,* 50 (Oct. 1951), 552-566.

Sultan, Stanley. "Call Me Ishmael: The Hagiography of Isaac McCaslin," *Texas Studies in Literature and Language,* 3 (Spring 1961), 50-66.

Trilling, Lionel. "The McCaslins of Mississippi," *Nation,* 154 (May 30, 1942), 632-633.

Warren, Robert Penn. "The Snopes World," *Kenyon Review,* 3 (Spring 1941), 253-257.

————. "William Faulkner," *William Faulkner: Three Decades*

of Criticism. East Lansing: Michigan State University Press, 1960. Pp.109-124. Originally published in *New Republic,* 115 (August 12, 1946), 176-180; continued (August 26, 1946), 234-237.

Wasiolek, Edward. *"As I Lay Dying:* Distortion in the Slow Eddy of Current Opinion," *Critique,* 3 (Spring-Fall 1959), 15-23.

Watkins, Floyd C. and Thomas Daniel Young. "Revisions of Style in Faulkner's *The Hamlet," Modern Fiction Studies,* 5 (Winter 1959-1960), 327-336.

Wheeler, Otis B. "Faulkner's Wilderness," *American Literature,* 31 (May 1959), 127-136.

"William C. Falkner," *Biographical and Historical Memoirs of Mississippi,* II. Chicago: Goodspeed, 1891. Pp.713-714.

Woodruff, Neal, Jr. " 'The Bear' and Faulkner's Moral Vision," *Studies in Faulkner.* Pittsburgh: Carnegie Institute of Technology, 1961. Pp.43-67.

Index

Important symbols and themes are indexed under separate entries (e.g., fire, light, death, love, flight, nostalgia, etc.). Relationships among characters or novels are indexed under "Patterns of relationships." Other items may generally be found under separate listing, titles of works, names of characters, or under "Faulkner."

Rousseau quote N. p168